UNAPOLOGETICALLY BROKEN

Spines

Unapologetically Broken

Inheritance of Pain with a Purified Soul

De'Angelo V. Tyler

In Loving Memory

Contents

Table of Contents

- **Chapter Four (Bitch Imma Crackbaby)**

Beware before you proceed to read this chapter. In this section of the novel we will learn about the author daddy issues and what is the attachment theory impact and how it has changed the author.

- **Chapter Five (Unmasking The Deceiver)**

I bet you did not know the author was a convict drug dealer. Continue reading and learn how I battled adversity and reclaimed my innocence.

- **Chapter Six (The Enemy Within)**

If you interested in what a Hero job description details than read this chapter to find out.

- **Chapter Seven (Fading Memories, Fading Powers)**

The author finds out what heart break truly feels like after losing his beloved Grandmother. Let us take a trip down memory lane as the author relive some of those dark moments.

- **Chapter Eight (Hero Mode: Activated)**

It is time for a history lesson. Let us travel through history and learn about substance abuse and alcohol addiction

- **Chapter Nine (Conclusion: The World Needs You)**

Sadly, all good things must come to a end. I hope you enjoyed your read and most importantly I hope you learned something. My advice to you, live your dreams and tell your story.

Acknowledgments

I would like to take a moment to express my heartfelt gratitude to those who have played a significant role in my life and have helped shape me into the person I am today.

First and foremost, I want to thank my father. Though you turned your back on me and left me to navigate this world on my own, I want you to know that your abandonment never diminished the love I have for you. It is a complex emotion, one that I have grappled with for years, but it is genuine, nonetheless. I hope that one day we can reconcile and that you can see the man I have become, despite your absence.

To my children, I do not even know where to begin. You are my everything – my reason for living, my breath of fresh air, my motivation for being the best version of myself. I love you more than words can express, and I am constantly inspired to be a great man for you and only you. I hope that one day you will carry the torch of changing the world, just as I have tried to do. You have the potential to achieve greatness, and I have no doubt that you will make a lasting impact on this world.

To my mother and stepfather, I want to express my deepest gratitude for the outstanding job you have done in raising me. Your love, support, and guidance have been invaluable, and I am forever in your debt. You have kept me focused, motivated, and driven, even when the road ahead seemed uncertain. I take my hat off to both of you – you have done an incredible job, and I could not be more thankful.

To my two brothers, I am so proud of the men you have become. I have had the privilege of watching you grow, evolve, and thrive, and I must say, I am impressed. You both have a bright future ahead of you, and I have no doubt that you will achieve great things. Keep pushing forward, keep striving for excellence, and never lose sight of your dreams.

To my entire family, I want to thank you for your unwavering love and support. You have been my rock, my safe haven, and my source of inspiration. Because of you, I have learned to represent our last name with pride, dignity, and honor. I hope that I have made you proud, and I look forward to continuing to make a positive impact on the world.

I would also like to extend my sincerest gratitude to Tajuddin Ministries, INC and Tajuddin Transformation Academy. Your tireless efforts to serve the community and transform the lives of those around you are truly inspiring. I am honored to be associated with your organization, and I look forward to seeing the incredible impact you will have on the hearts of the people.

To our ancestors, who paved the way for us to be here today, I offer my deepest gratitude. Your sacrifices, struggles, and triumphs have not gone unnoticed. We stand on your shoulders, and we continue to push forward, fueled by your legacy.

To the black leaders, past and present, who have fought tirelessly for our freedom, equality, and justice, I salute you. Your courage, resilience, and determination have inspired generations, and we continue to draw strength from your examples.

To those who have marched, protested, and fought for our rights, often in the face of overwhelming oppression, death, and violence, I thank you. Your sacrifices and all the ass whoppings you all took on our behave will not go in vain, and we honor your memory by continuing to push forward, demanding a better world for ourselves and for future generations.

Finally, I want to express my gratitude to all the individuals and organizations out there who are fighting for a better world. You are the unsung heroes, the ones who often go unnoticed, but whose contributions are invaluable. You are the change-makers, the trailblazers, and the pioneers. Keep pushing forward, keep fighting for justice, equality, and freedom. You are the superheroes of our time, and I am honored to stand alongside you in this fight.

Unapologetically Broken

Inheritance of Pain with a Purified Soul

De'Angelo V. Tyler

About the Author

Who I Am

Born and raised on the South Side of Chicago, De'Angelo V. Tyler's journey is one defined by dedication, resilience, and a deep commitment to bettering the lives of those around him. His upbringing in a vibrant but often challenging community shaped his values of family, friendship, and community service —values that have guided his professional and personal endeavors.

Early Life and Education

De'Angelo's academic achievements began early, graduating as a member of the National Honors Society from Chicago Public Schools. This accomplishment reflected his determination to excel despite the challenges of urban life. Education was more than just a pathway for De'Angelo; it was a means to uplift his community and create opportunities for himself and others.

Pursuing higher education, De'Angelo earned a degree in Liberal Arts and Social Services, a field that resonated deeply with his passion for serving others. Not content with stopping there, he is now working toward another degree in Mental Health Counseling, demonstrating his belief in lifelong learning and his desire to expand his impact in the realm of mental health.

A Career in Law Enforcement

De'Angelo's professional journey began in law enforcement, where he spent over 11 years, primarily in Corrections and Work Release facilities. His work in this field was more than a job—it was a calling to ensure safety, support rehabilitation, and uphold justice. Throughout this period, De'Angelo developed a profound understanding of human behavior, resilience, and the power of second chances. He approached his role with a blend of authority and compassion, recognizing the humanity in every individual he met.

This experience also taught him invaluable lessons about leadership, crisis management, and the importance of creating pathways for those seeking redemption. It laid a solid foundation for his later work in social services and recovery.

Social Services and Community Outreach

After more than a decade in law enforcement, De'Angelo transitioned into the field of social services, where he has dedicated over six years to community outreach and support. His work has focused on connecting individuals and families to resources that improve their quality of life, address systemic barriers, and foster self-sufficiency.

De'Angelo's efforts in community outreach have been deeply rooted in his belief that every individual deserves dignity, respect, and access to opportunities. From mentoring young people to organizing programs for underserved populations, his impact has been both broad and personal. His ability to build trust and inspire hope has made him a pillar in the communities he serves.

Building Expertise in Counseling and Coaching

In addition to his work in social services, De'Angelo has pursued extensive certifications to enhance his ability to support others. As a certified Life Coach, Health Coach, Relationship Coach, Teen Life Coach, Kids Life Coach, ADHD Coach, LGBTQ Coach, and more, he has developed a versatile skill set to meet the diverse needs of his clients. His dedication to obtaining these credentials reflects his commitment to being a well-rounded and effective resource for people navigating life's challenges.

De'Angelo has also earned licenses in Wisconsin, Indiana, Ohio, and Illinois as a Substance and Alcohol Abuse Counselor, further expanding his ability to address critical issues affecting individuals and families. His goal is to practice throughout the Midwest, bringing his expertise to communities in need and creating a regional impact.

Recovery and Housing Solutions

Expanding his reach even further, De'Angelo has embarked on a second career focused on recovery and housing solutions. By operating sober, transitional, and long-term living housing, he provides a lifeline for individuals looking to rebuild their lives. These facilities are more than just places to stay; they are environments where residents can heal, grow, and rediscover their potential.

De'Angelo's work in this area is grounded in his belief that recovery is not a one-size-fits-all journey. By creating supportive and flexible housing solutions, he empowers individuals to take control of their futures while fostering a sense of community and accountability.

A Global Perspective: Humanitarian and Volunteer Work

De'Angelo's commitment to service extends far beyond his local community. He has traveled extensively, engaging in humanitarian and volunteer work both domestically and internationally. These experiences have broadened his perspective, deepened his empathy, and reinforced his belief in the interconnectedness of all people.

From disaster relief efforts to educational initiatives in underserved regions, De'Angelo's global contributions reflect his unwavering dedication to making a difference wherever he goes. His travels have not only enriched his understanding of the world but also informed his approach to service, blending cultural sensitivity with practical solutions.

Looking Ahead: Vision and Aspirations

As De'Angelo continues to expand his professional expertise and community impact, his vision stays clear: to be a catalyst for change in the Midwest and beyond. Whether through counseling, coaching, recovery programs, or humanitarian efforts, he is committed to empowering individuals to overcome obstacles and achieve their full potential.

De'Angelo's journey is a testament to the power of perseverance, education, and a heart dedicated to service. He embodies the belief that by lifting others, we elevate ourselves, creating a ripple effect that transforms communities and inspires future generations.

Introduction

"There is no better teacher than adversity. Every defeat, every heartbreak, every loss, contains its own seed, its own lesson on how to improve your performance the next time".
—Malcolm X

I never imagined my life would take this path. Born into a world where addiction and chaos is normal, I found myself standing at a crossroads—one path leading toward destruction, the other toward redemption. I chose redemption, but not just for myself. I made a vow to help others escape the grip of substance abuse and alcohol addiction, to fight for those who felt forgotten, and to dedicate my life to making a difference.

This book is not just my story—it is a testament to survival, resilience, and transformation. It is a journey through the highs and lows of my life, woven together with the stories of those I have loved, lost, and fought for. It is the story of a child abandoned by my father, a boy raised in the shadow of addiction, and a man who refused to let his past define his future.

Substance abuse is not just an individual struggle; it is a generational curse, passed down like an heirloom no one wants but so many inherit. I saw it firsthand. My father was consumed by addiction, in and out of prison, missing from my life for over thirty years. His absence left a void, a question I spent decades trying to answer: Why? Why wasn't I enough? Why did drugs hold more power over him than his own child? These questions haunted me, shaping the way I viewed myself and the world around me.

My grandmother, too, wrestled with the demons of alcohol. I have vivid memories of her, some warm and full of love, others clouded by the haze of intoxication. She was a woman of strength, but even the strongest among us can fall victim to addiction. Watching her struggle planted the first seeds of my mission.

I grew up surrounded by addiction, yet I never let it consume me. Instead, I became an observer, a student of the chaos unfolding around me. I watched as friends and family members lost themselves to the bottle, to the pipe, to the needle. I saw how substance abuse destroyed relationships, shattered families, and stole futures. But I also saw something else hope.

Hope in the resilience of those who fought to get clean. Hope in the stories of redemption, of people who clawed their way back from the depths of addiction. Hope in my own ability to rise above my circumstances and become a voice for change.

This book is a reflection of that journey. It is an honest, unfiltered account of my life, the battles I have fought, and the lessons I have learned. It is about the impact of addiction on Black and Brown communities, how political policies—especially those introduced by Presidents Nixon, Reagan, and Clinton—waged war not just on drugs but on the people who used them. The so-called "War on Drugs" was never about saving lives; it was about control, about criminalizing Black and Brown bodies while turning a blind eye to the root causes of addiction.

I explore the science of addiction through the lens of attachment theory, examining how early childhood experiences shape our ability to form healthy relationships and cope with trauma. I share my personal experiences with false accusations, with the criminal justice system that sought to brand me as a drug dealer, only for me to later work in law enforcement, helping those society had given up on.

Traveling across the country and around the world opened my eyes to the universal nature of addiction. No matter where I went, I saw the same pain in different faces. Substance abuse does not discriminate—it affects all races, religions, and socioeconomic backgrounds. But what does change is the way society responds. In wealthy communities, addiction is treated as a public health crisis. In Black and Brown communities, it is treated as a crime.

Faith has played a significant role in my journey. As a Muslim, I have turned to the teachings of Islam for guidance and strength. I reflect on the profound concept that angels address a fetus while in the womb, speaking its destiny into existence. It is a reminder that from the very beginning, we are seen, known, and given purpose. My purpose, I have come to understand, is to fight—to advocate, to educate, to heal.

I do not claim to have all the answers, but I do have experience, passion, and an unwavering belief that recovery is possible for anyone willing to do the work. In this book, I share not just my own story but practical steps for those looking to break free from addiction. I discuss how to become a counselor, how to develop effective treatment plans, and how we, as a society, can do better in supporting those who struggle.

To those who have battled addiction, who have lost loved

ones, who have felt the sting of judgment and the weight of stigma—you are not alone. Your past does not define you, and your future is still yours to write.

To those who have never experienced addiction firsthand but want to understand, to help, to be part of the solution—thank you. Awareness is the first step toward change, and change is desperately needed.

This book is for the forgotten, the misunderstood, the incarcerated, the recovering, the relapsing, and the reborn. It is for those still fighting and for those who believe in second chances.

I wrote this book because I refuse to be silent. I refuse to let my father's addiction, my grandmother's struggles, my false arrest, or the statistics about Black and Brown communities be just another sad story. I am here to rewrite the narrative.

I am here to tell the truth, to expose the systems that profit off of addiction while punishing the addicted. I am here to show that healing is possible, that redemption is real, and that no one is beyond saving.

I am here because I have seen the worst of addiction—and I have seen the best of recovery.

This is my story. But more than that, this is a call to action.

So, are you ready to listen?

What It Feels Like

As the craving intensifies, rational thought dissolves, replaced by an overwhelming urge to escape. The substance beckons, promising temporary reprieve from emotional pain, stress, or anxiety. Users convince themselves they need it to cope, forgetting past regrets and broken promises.

With each dose, a fleeting sense of euphoria masks underlying issues. The substance becomes an emotional crutch, silencing inner turmoil. Addicts rationalize their dependence, downplaying consequences and manipulating loved ones to enable their habit.

As addiction tightens its grip, self-awareness fades. Users disconnect from their values, relationships, and aspirations. Shame and guilt accumulate, fueling further substance abuse in a vicious cycle. Inner conflict rages: desperation to quit versus overwhelming withdrawal fears.

In rare moments of clarity, reality pierces the haze. Users glimpse shattered dreams, damaged relationships, and lost potential. A glimmer of determination appears, sparking hopes of recovery. But without support and resilience, the cycle often persists, obscuring the path to redemption.

Drugs and alcohol addiction originates in the brain's reward system, which regulates pleasure, motivation, and learning. This complex network involves structures like the ventral tegmental area (VTA), nucleus accumbens (NAcc) and prefrontal cortex (PFC). Normally, the reward system responds to natural pleasures like food, sex, and social interactions.

When an individual uses drugs and alcohol they trigger an intense release of dopamine, a neurotransmitter associated with pleasure and reward. Dopamine floods the NAcc, creating a euphoric sensation. This rapid dopamine surge reinforces drug-seeking and drinking behavior.

Repeated drug and alcohol use leads to tolerance, where the brain adapts by reducing dopamine receptors. To achieve the same high, users increase dosage or frequency. When drug levels drop, withdrawal symptoms appear, driven by dopamine depletion.

Chronic drug and alcohol exposure alters brain structure and function. The VTA and NAcc shrink, while stress circuits expand. This reorganization compromises decision-making, impulse control, and emotional regulation.

Drug-induced dopamine release strengthens synaptic

connections through long-term potentiation (LTP). This process solidifies drug-associated memories, making cravings more persistent.

Alcohol affects neurotransmitters GABA (inhibitory) and glutamate (excitatory). Initially, GABA increases, inducing relaxation. Long-term use disrupts balance, leading to anxiety, tremors, and seizures.

Stress activates the brain's stress response, releasing corticotropin-releasing factor (CRF). CRF increases dopamine release, triggering cravings. Stress becomes a significant relapse trigger.

Drug and alcohol addiction disrupts neurotransmitter balance. Dopamine, serotonin, and GABA levels fluctuate, affecting mood, motivation, and impulse control. This imbalance perpetuates addiction.

Recovery requires reversing these neural adaptations. Medications and therapies aim to restore dopamine balance, reduce cravings, and strengthen cognitive control. Behavioral interventions help rebuild reward system functioning, promoting long-term recovery.

Chapter 1

___

From Zero to Hero

In Islam, it is believed that during a woman's pregnancy, within the first 120 days of conception the angel's visit is a pivotal moment in the development of the fetus, marking the beginning of its journey towards becoming a living, breathing being.

As the angel approaches the fetus, it is said that the fetus is surrounded by a warm, comforting light. This light is a manifestation of Allah's mercy and compassion and serves as a reminder of the love and care that Allah has for all of His creations.

The angel's first task is to breathe life into the fetus. This is done through a gentle, whispery breath that awakens the fetus to its surroundings. As the angel breathes life into the fetus, it is said that the fetus begins to stir, its tiny heart beating with a newfound sense of purpose.

Once the fetus has been given life, the angel begins to shape and mold it into the person it will become. This is a delicate and intricate process, one that requires great care and attention to detail. The angel must carefully craft the fetus's physical form, ensuring that it is strong and healthy.

But the angel's task goes far beyond the physical realm. It is also responsible for imparting to the fetus its unique personality, talents, and abilities. This is a mysterious and wondrous process, one that is guided by Allah's infinite wisdom and knowledge.

As the angel works to shape and mold the fetus, it is said that the fetus begins to take on a life of its own. It starts to move and kick, its tiny limbs stretching out as it explores its surroundings. This is a magical and awe-inspiring moment, one that fills the heart with joy and wonder.

The angel's visit is not just a one-time event, but rather an ongoing process that continues throughout the pregnancy. The angel remains with the fetus, guiding and protecting it as it grows and develops.

As the pregnancy progresses, the angel continues to impart its wisdom and knowledge to the fetus. It teaches the fetus about the world around it which helps it to understand its place in the universe. This is a truly remarkable process, one that is full of wonder and awe.

The angel's presence is a reminder of Allah's infinite love and mercy. It is a testament to the care and compassion that Allah has for all of His creations, and a reminder of the sacred trust that has been placed in us as parents.

As the angel completes its task and the fetus is born, it is said that the angel remains with the child, guiding and protecting it throughout its life. This is a truly beautiful and comforting thought, one that fills the heart with peace and tranquility.

"My arrival was, to put it mildly, a momentous occasion. Imagine the hushed anticipation, the air thick with expectation. It was as if the universe held its breath, waiting for the unveiling of something extraordinary. And then, I entered the world.

I would not say I was a breath of fresh air but more like a hammer to the solar plexus. The medical staff, seasoned professionals though they were, were visibly awestruck. My first cry, a powerful and resonant sound, echoed through the delivery room, a proclamation of my arrival. Picture the trumpets of Louis Armstrong playing his favorite tune over and over again. It was clear, even then, that I was no ordinary child.

My parents, their faces a mixture of wonder and awe, gazed down at me. They understood, instinctively, that they had been entrusted with something special. The weight of this realization, the responsibility of nurturing a child destined for greatness, was palpable.

From the very beginning, I was a captivating presence. My coos were melodic, my laughter infectious. Nurses would gather around my crib, captivated by my charm and intelligence. I was aware, even then, of the impact I had on others.

You might think I am being boastful, but I am simply stating the truth. I was not just a child; I was something more. I was a unique individual, born with a purpose, with a destiny to fulfill.

My parents, in their own way, helped cultivate this understanding. They would share stories of my early childhood most memorable moments which was often not good, my remarkable intelligence, and my infectious enthusiasm. I would listen, a gentle smile playing on my lips, knowing that I was indeed special.

As a child, sometimes we don't see past the playground, video games and the cute girls in the neighborhood it is complicated being a gifted child. I wanted to be a force of nature, a whirlwind of creativity and ambition. I was driven to make a difference, to leave my mark on the world. And I will. My journey has just begun, and I am ready to embrace it, to face any challenge in order to achieve greatness.

At times, my childhood often felt like a comic book story filled with daring feats, personal battles, and unwavering loyalty to those I cared about. In many ways, my young life mirrored the life of Daredevil, the superhero whose dual roles as protector and misfit defined his existence. Like him, I spent much of my youth fighting battles some visible, some hidden. And while I found strength in my athletic gifts and fierce sense of duty, I often wonder how much farther I could have gone if I had more support, especially from my father.

From the earliest days I can remember, I saw myself as a protector. Much like Daredevil's commitment to safeguarding Hell's Kitchen, I took it upon myself to defend my brothers and other family members. Amongst my peers I was one of the oldest with that came responsible that I did not sign up for but who am I to question God's plan. Between me and you, some-times I did not act like I was. Like most of us I did a lot of stupid shit and honestly if I could do it all over again, I would definitely not change anything.

Especially the time I was in either preschool or kinder-garten I stole my teacher car keys. Now before yo ass starting judging me I need you to hear me out. My teacher was this short, tiny white haired which looking bitch (excuse my language). Her attitude and choice of word stuck a nerve with me every time, truthfully she was a sweet old lady I just did not like her. I do not know why I took her car keys but if I had to guess me not liking her was definitely the reason.

My second grade teacher was probably my first woman crush ever. She broke my heart when I received a detention notice. I was mortified at the thought of showing it to my mother, knowing that it would lead to a routine ass whooping. In a moment of misguided ingenuity, I decided to take matters into my own hands. I concocted a plan to forge my mother's signature on the detention notice, hoping to avoid her wrath.

However, my 2nd-grade teacher was not so easily deceived. She scrutinized the signature, her eyes narrowing as she detected the obvious forgery. I was caught red-handed, and my teacher wasted no time in contacting my mother. I was devastated had I not been in love with her I swear ain't no telling what I would have done to her ass to.

As expected, my mother was furious when she discovered the truth. I took my ass whooping with pride. To this day, I still harbor a hint of resentment towards my 2nd-grade teacher for exposing my deception. While I acknowledge that she was simply doing her job, a part of me wish that bitch (excuse my language) would have just let the shit go.

One last fun memorable time was the time I push one of my summer school teacher somewhat down the stairs for being a bitch (excuse my language) but she deserved that shit. Unlike the first teacher I victimized, my third grade teacher was a piece of work definitely the worst teacher I ever had. I would soon quickly learn a life lesson and that was do not fuck around in school because they will fail yo ass thank god I did not expelled from school. Even though I was wrong I do not think my actions should have resulted in me having to repeat the third grade again.

I do however wish I had better elementary school years, I recall a journey marked by academic challenges. Despite my best efforts, I struggled to keep up with my peers, consistently earning grades that hovered around the C and D range. Occasional glimpses of hope appeared in the form of a rare B, but unfortunately, these moments were often offset by a disappointing F.

My struggles in the classroom were multifaceted, with reading, math, and comprehension proving to be particularly daunting subjects. I remember feeling overwhelmed by the complexity of math problems and the seemingly endless stream of reading assignments. My inability to grasp these fundamental concepts left me feeling frustrated and defeated.

Despite my struggles, I was fortunate to have teachers who, although perhaps not enthusiastic about my academic prospects, nonetheless provided me with the support and guidance I needed to navigate the challenges of elementary school. In retrospect, I realize that their patience and dedication were instrumental in helping me to persevere, even when my academic performance was less than stellar.

In a humorous, yet poignant, analogy, I often joke that if elementary school were akin to professional sports, I would have been the player who was perpetually on the trading block. My academic struggles would have made me a less-than-desirable asset, and I likely would have found myself as a free agent, struggling to find a team willing to take a chance on me. Despite these challenges, I am grateful for the lessons learned during those formative years, which have served as a foundation for my future growth and success.

It was not often I had to step in between my younger brothers but when I did I enjoyed fighting. God is my witness I enjoyed spending the night at my cousins house and in the projects (a sixteen story housing complex) because a wanted to play hood vigilante and seek revenge on the group of bullies that targeted my cousins. My mom probably was just happy yo get rid of my ass for the weekend thinking I was behaving myself but in fact we was running the hallway just young kids jeopardizing losing our innocence. I was always the first to stand up. I embraced that role with a fierce sense of responsibility. Every punch I threw, every insult hurled my way felt like a badge of honor because it meant I would spare someone else from harm.

But that same defiance that made me a protector also got me into plenty of trouble. School, for me, was less about academics and more about battles literal and figurative. Like Daredevil often finding himself on the wrong side of the law while fighting for justice, I often found myself on the wrong side of school authority. I was suspended more times than I can count, and detention felt like my second home. It was not that I enjoyed breaking the rules; it was that I could not sit idly by when something was not right or if my teachers would not let me have my way. If someone was being mistreated, I intervened, no matter the consequences to this day that is still my approach.

Despite my issues with authority, I excelled in sports. My athleticism was undeniable a natural gift that earned me respect, even from those who might not have liked me otherwise. On the basketball court, football field, or even in impromptu neighborhood games, I shone. I could jump higher, run faster, and play harder than anyone around me. My physical abilities were my superpower, much like Daredevil's heightened senses. It was not just skill; it was instinct a drive to push myself to the limit every time I played.

In the neighborhood, my athleticism elevated my reputation. Older kids who once dismissed me as just another scrappy kid began to take notice. I was no longer just the troublemaker who got suspended or the kid who fought for his brothers—I was a force to be reckoned with. I became a fixture in neighborhood games, always the one people wanted on their team when the stakes were high. It was a taste of the respect I craved, a validation of my worth that school could not provide.

Looking back, I often think about how far I could have gone with my athletic talent. I was not good—I was exceptional. I genuinely believe I could have been a professional athlete if things had been different. But the truth is, I did not have the support system I needed to reach that level, especially from my father. My step father was present in our home, but not in the ways I needed him to be. He was not the kind of man to cheer from the sidelines or push me to train harder. He was not the one to tell me, "You can do this," or to guide me toward the opportunities that could have turned my talent into a career. He did attend more sporting events did my mother, I respected him for the little he did in that aspect of my life but let us be honest it should have been my own lousy ass biological father doing that. Might I add, my stepfather is a awesome man and deserves all the credit for taking on that role he did the best he could.

I do not hold anger toward my father—at least, not anymore. I know he had his own struggles and limitations, and he thought he was doing his best. But I cannot help but wonder how different my life might have been if he had been more involved along side my stepfather. If he had been the one to take me to practice, to encourage me after a tough game, or to sit me down and help me plan for a future in sports, my story would have had a different ending.

Instead, I had to find my own way. My mother supported me as best as she could, but raising a family was not easy for her, especially with me constantly being sent home from school or getting into fights. She saw the potential in me but did not always have the tools to help me channel it. I carried a lot of frustration in those days—anger at the world for not giving me the opportunities I deserved and anger at myself for not knowing how to create those opportunities on my own.

Despite it all, my childhood taught me resilience. Every fight, every detention, every hard-fought game taught me something about strength—both physical and emotional. Like Daredevil, navigating the tightrope between his role as a protector and the challenges of his personal life, I learned to walk the line between success and struggle. And while I never made it to the professional leagues, I can still look back with pride on the respect I earned and the battles I fought.

Even now, as an adult, I carry the lessons of my childhood with me. I am still a protector at heart, still someone who stands up for what is right, even when it is not easy.

I still feel the fire of competition and the thrill of physical achievement, even if it is no longer on a court or field. And I still believe in the power of resilience—the ability to rise after every fall, to fight back against every challenge.

But there is always that lingering question: What if? What if I had the support I needed? What if my father had been more present in my journey? I do not dwell on it as much as I used to, but it is a question that will always stay with me. Because while I am proud of who I have become, I know I had the potential to be so much more.

CHAPTER 2

THERE IS NO TURNING BACK

<u>JOURNEY</u>

noun

1. an act of traveling from one place to another.

    "He went on a long journey"

A journey is far more profound than merely traveling from one place to another. It is an exploration a process of navigating through experiences, emotions, and challenges. Some journeys take the form of physical travel, like venturing to a distant land. Others are deeply personal and metaphorical, such as growing as an individual, uncovering intellectual truths, or pursuing spiritual enlightenment. At its heart, every journey is about transformation whether of the mind, body, or spirit.

The reasons behind embarking on a journey are as diverse as the people who undertake them. For some, including myself, a journey is an escape a way to break free from the monotony or pressures of daily life. For others, it is a quest for something greater a pursuit of knowledge, connection, or a deeper sense of purpose. Sometimes, journeys are not chosen but imposed by life's circumstances an unexpected event that force us to grow, adapt, and change. Whatever the reason, the purpose of a journey is always deeply personal, often understood fully only in hindsight.

The solitude of a journey is a transformative experience that has been undertaken by many of the world's most revered leaders, prophets, and superheroes. Jesus Christ, for example, spent 40 days in the desert, while Malcolm X traveled to the desert to discover his purpose. Many others, including Moses and Muhammad, have also ventured into the wilderness to seek guidance and wisdom. Similarly, superheroes often begin their journey in solitude, discovering their superpowers and learning to harness them for the greater good.

Now, just because the wilderness has been the proven ground for revaluation and enlightenment, that does mean you should take your ass into a dessert and think you will gain some type of secret powers or spiritual enlightenment. In fact, if not properly monitored you will find yourself on what is called a suicide mission and your stupid ass will more likely die it is as simple as that. However, we should look more into understanding our journey. For this will ensure we have a sense of direction and a purpose to reach our destination.

These journeys are not merely physical, but also spiritual and emotional. They require the individual to step outside of their familiar surroundings, to confront their deepest fears, and to learn to overcome adversity. The solitude of the journey provides a unique opportunity for introspection, self-reflection, and spiritual growth. It is a time for the individual to connect with their inner self, to discover their purpose, and to clarify their values.

I am sure we all know this journey is not an easy one, however. It is fraught with challenges, obstacles, and uncertainties. We must learn to navigate through uncharted territories, to find creative solutions to unexpected problems, and to persevere in the face of adversity. The journey tests our resolve, our courage, and our character. It pushes us to our limits, forcing us to confront our deepest fears and to overcome them.

Despite the challenges, the journey is a transformative experience that enables the us to discover our true potential. It is a time of growth, of learning, and of self-discovery. We must appear from our solitude with a newfound sense of purpose, a clearer understanding of our core values, and a deeper connection to our inner self. We than will start to become more stronger, wiser, and more resilient, ready to face the challenges of the world.

When we finally muster the courage to be ourselves, we often face a daunting reality of loneliness. It is as if the world around us is designed to encourage conformity, and those who dare to be different are left to navigate the challenges of self-discovery alone. Soon we will notice how everyone around us seems to want to fit in, to be like everyone else, or to become someone they are not. But when we choose to break free from the mold and forge our own path, we are often met with resistance, criticism, and ultimately loneliness.

However, it is precisely this loneliness that can become a catalyst for growth and self-discovery. When we are no longer bound by the need to conform, we are free to explore our true passions, values, and desires. We begin to uncover our unique strengths and talents, and we start to pursue our dreams with renewed purpose and determination.

Yes, the journey can be lonely at times, but it is also incredibly liberating. As we continue to grow and evolve into our authentic selves, we will find that the loneliness gives way to a deeper sense of connection with ourselves and the world around us. We will discover that being different is not something to be feared, but something to be celebrated, and that our uniqueness is the very thing that makes us truly special.

Here is the darker side, at the beginning of every journey there is a vision that guides and motivates us to keep moving forward. This vision is truly us discovering our why. However, it is a peculiar truth that our vision can only have one true believer which is the one who has that vision. It is not wise to believe anyone will believe in your vision because that is not how life works. The reason for this is because the vision is often born out of a unique combination of experiences, passions, and values that are specific to the individual. As a result, the journey to achieving that vision can be a lonely one, as others may not fully understand or share the same level of commitment to the vision.

But here is the good news, in my experience people are often drawn to those who are unwavering in their commitment to their vision, even if it means embracing loneliness. When we demonstrate that we are willing to pursue our vision, regardless of the cost, we become more attractive to others who are inspired by our passion and conviction. In fact, it is precisely our aloneness that can become a magnet for others, as they are drawn to the confidence and clarity that comes from staying true to our vision. By embracing our aloneness and staying committed to our vision, soon you will no longer alone.

Leaders are often lonely figures, standing at the forefront of their endeavors with no one by their side. We are the ones who venture into uncharted territory, who take the first step into the unknown, and who bear the weight of responsibility for our decisions. This can be an isolating experience, as we are often forced to rely solely on our own judgment and intuition. But this loneliness is not a coincidence - it is a deliberate choice that we must make as leaders. While pursuing your vision I would not recommend you to surround your with people because when we surround ourselves with others, we risk becoming part of the crowd, losing our unique perspective and our ability to lead.

The irony is that we leaders often choose this loneliness, recognizing that it is a necessary part of our journey. We understand that in order to change the world, we must be willing to stand apart from it. This is the greatest test of our resolve, the moment of truth that separates the true leaders from the pretenders. Choosing to be alone is not an easy decision, but it is a crucial one. It requires us to be self-reliant, to trust our own instincts, and to have the courage to forge our own path. And it is precisely this loneliness that ultimately enables us to achieve greatness, to make a lasting impact on the world, and to leave a legacy that will outlast us.

In Islamic history a pivotal event took place, this event occurred in 621 CE. Isra'wa-Mi'raj better known as The Night Journey is a miraculous journey taken by Prophet Muhammad. On the 27th of Rajab, Prophet Muhammad was in the holy city of Mecca. There, he was praying at the Kaaba. Suddenly, he was approached by the angel Jibril (Gabriel), who came in the form of a man. Jibril awoke Prophet Muhammad and split open his chest to cleanse his heart. Jibril removed Prophet Muhammad's heart, washed it with Zamzam water and filled it with faith and wisdom. This purification prepared Prophet Muhammad for his spiritual journey. After the purification, Jibril led Prophet Muhammad to a white winged horse named Buraq. The Buraq was taller than a donkey but smaller than a mule, with wings on its sides.

Prophet Muhammad mounted Buraq, and they set off towards the heavens. Along the way, they stopped at various locations, and visited the graves of previous prophets, where Prophet Muhammad led them in prayer. The city of Bethlehem, where Prophet Muhammad prayed. Upon arriving in Jerusalem, Prophet Muhammad dismounted Buraq and tied it to the Western Wall of the Temple Mount. He then entered the Dome of the Rock and prayed alongside other prophets, including Abraham, Moses, and Jesus.

After prayer, Prophet Muhammad ascended to the heavens on a ladder of light, accompanied by Jibril. They passed through seven levels of heaven, meeting various prophets and witnessing wonders. Prophet Muhammad reached the highest heaven, where he met Allah and received revelations.

During this encounter, Allah ordained the five daily prayers for Muslims. Prophet Muhammad descended from the heavens and returned to Jerusalem. He mounted Buraq and rode back to Mecca. The entire journey took place in a single night, and Prophet Muhammad returned to Mecca before dawn. This miraculous journey demonstrated the true meaning of steeping out on faith.

In case you have not figured it out yet, the heart is considered the sacred center of an individual's being, where intentions, emotions, and spiritual awareness converge. The heart is not just a physical organ, but a metaphysical entity that harbors the deepest secrets of a person's soul. It is the seat of intention, where thoughts, feelings, and desires are shaped, and from which all actions and decisions emanate.

The Quran emphasizes the importance of the heart, stating, "Indeed, it is not the eyes that are blind, but it is the hearts in the chests that are blind" (22:46). This highlights the crucial role the heart plays in perceiving reality, making decisions, and navigating life's challenges. By cultivating a pure, sincere, and compassionate heart, one can align their intentions with divine guidance, leading to a life of purpose, wisdom, and spiritual growth.

In 2010 I return home from college, if I am not mistaken it was for summer break. Back home in Chicago for the first time in my life I felt lost, a culture shock was taking place. The Night Journey holds immense significance in Islam it demonstrates Prophet Muhammad's prophethood, establishes the importance of Jerusalem in Islam, emphasizes the unity of prophets, reinforces the obligation of daily prayers.

Make no mistake about it, I am nothing like Prophet Muhammad nor do I have all of his attributes. However, I do learn from his teaching and try my hardest to implement his examples of being the best I can be in my everyday life. My global journey helping individuals overcome substance abuse, alcohol addiction and guiding them toward holistic wellness through coaching and counseling. I am reminded of Prophet Muhammad's miraculous Night Journey. But my personal journey does not even come close to that of Isra'wa-Mi'raj.

Just as Allah took Prophet Muhammad on a transformative spiritual journey, I feel divine guidance on my own path. Allah has led me through 27 states and over 20 countries, broadening my understanding and compassion. This world is not what we think it is, there is so much more to it. Beneath the veneer of

Instagram-perfect landscapes, flawless faces, and captivating treasures, lies a complex tapestry of untold stories, hidden struggles, and profound mysteries waiting to be unraveled.

America has countless places where alcohol and drug use are not only tolerated but openly encouraged as part of the culture. Cities like Las Vegas, New Orleans, and Miami thrive on nonstop partying, with bars and clubs promoting excessive drinking 24/7. In these places, public intoxication is seen as just another part of the experience, and people walk the streets with open containers, sometimes barely able to stand. Music festivals, tailgate parties, and spring break destinations across the country create environments where alcohol consumption is constant, and drug use—particularly party drugs like ecstasy, cocaine, and marijuana—is common. While law enforcement may crack down on certain substances, there is an undeniable double standard when it comes to how society views alcohol abuse compared to other forms of substance use.

Beyond the nightlife and party scenes, the normalization of drug and alcohol use extends into everyday American culture. In some cities, cannabis dispensaries operate openly, making marijuana as accessible as a cup of coffee, while other drugs like psychedelics are gaining acceptance in certain states. Meanwhile, prescription drug abuse remains a widespread but often overlooked problem, with opioids, stimulants, and benzodiazepines frequently misused behind closed doors. College campuses, corporate events, and even upscale social gatherings often involve heavy drinking, sometimes paired with cocaine or other stimulants to keep the energy going. Despite this, addiction is still stigmatized—unless it is happening in an environment where people can afford to hide it. The reality is, America has created a culture where substance use for pleasure and fun is widely accepted in certain settings, but when addiction takes hold in lower-income communities, it is met with criminalization and judgment rather than treatment and understanding.

As I have traveled abroad, I have noticed that some countries have a significantly higher drug use culture compared to the United States. In certain regions, it is not uncommon to see drugs and alcohol being used openly and freely, often as a way to complement social gatherings and celebrations. This cultural normalization of drug use can be jarring for American visitors, who may be more accustomed to the strict laws and stigma surrounding drug use in the US.

In many of these countries, poverty and homelessness are rampant, and the drug market often thrives at the expense of vulnerable populations. I have seen firsthand how desperation and lack of opportunities can drive individuals to turn to drugs as a means of escape or coping mechanism. It is heartbreaking to witness, and it highlights the need for comprehensive social and economic support systems to address the root causes of poverty and addiction.

Visiting Tokyo, Japan, was truly the greatest travel experience of my life. The city was filled with hardworking, respectful citizens, and I was amazed by how clean and safe it felt. Everywhere I went, from the bustling streets of Shibuya to the quiet neighborhoods of Meguro, there was a sense of order and discipline that I had never quite experienced anywhere else. Now, do not get me wrong—I am sure there are areas that local Japanese citizens might have advised me to avoid. But let's be real, I'm from Chicago's South Side. I've seen and been through some serious things, so it takes a lot to rattle me. Despite that, Tokyo felt different. It was the kind of place where I could walk at night without constantly looking over my shoulder, and that in itself was an experience worth remembering.

One thing that stood out to me the most was the absence of

visible homelessness and public smoking. I do not recall ever seeing someone sleeping on the trains, lying in front of a store, or even smoking a cigarette in public. The youth were incredibly well-behaved, and even during after-school hours, I did not see kids vaping or smoking anything. It was almost surreal. Studies have shown that places with high drug usage often have high crime rates, including missing children and cases of child abuse. Seeing so many children in Tokyo confidently navigating the city alone—grocery shopping, walking to and from school without parents, and simply enjoying their childhood without fear—only reinforced that claim. The level of public safety and discipline in Japan is something I deeply respect, and it made my visit all the more unforgettable.

Visiting Havana, Cuba, was an eye-opening experience, and in my opinion, it was the poorest country I had ever seen. Now, I grew up in some rough areas, but compared to Cuba, those neighborhoods felt like luxury. This isn't to say that I have a deep understanding of the country's economy or inner workings, but just based on what I saw on the surface level, life there seemed tough. Walking through the streets, I noticed how old and worn down many of the buildings were, how resources seemed scarce, and how people made do with very little. You would think that living in such conditions would make people angry, bitter, or even desperate enough to turn to crime just to support a drug habit. But to my surprise, that wasn't the case at all.

The Cuban people were some of the friendliest and most welcoming people I had ever been around. Despite their struggles, they did not let their conditions consume them. Everyone I encountered was hardworking and incredibly respectful. They definitely knew how to party, and I saw plenty of people enjoying beers and other drinks, but what stood out to me was that I didn't see a single person who looked strung out on drugs. There were no homeless people sleeping on the streets, no signs of addiction taking over the community like in so many other places I've been. It was almost unreal. Seeing how resilient and joyful the people were, even in the face of poverty, made this one of the most rewarding trips I have ever taken.

Visiting Europe was an interesting experience, especially given the stories I had heard about the continent's drug crisis. However, during my time there, nothing really stood out to me in terms of widespread drug use or homelessness. Compared to what I have seen in America, it seemed like European countries had a much better handle on these issues. I expected to see signs of drug addiction and poverty in London, but to my surprise, the city was remarkably clean and well-maintained. London itself was absolutely beautiful, with its historic architecture, diverse culture, and vibrant energy. If I ever decided to move abroad, London would definitely be high on my list of places to live.

Paris was no different—nothing about the city screamed "drug crisis" to me. I walked through different neighborhoods, visited popular tourist attractions, and even stopped to ask a local for directions to a nearby cigar lounge. The man I spoke to casually mentioned that if I was looking for "good stuff," I would have better luck at clubs or after-hour spots. That was the first real indication I got that drugs were present, but even then, it wasn't in my face like in some American cities. Italy and Barcelona were much the same. I didn't see open-air drug markets, people strung out on the streets, or large homeless encampments. Of course, every place has its issues, but from what I observed, Europe seemed to have far better control over its drug and homelessness problems than the U.S.

Despite the challenges posed by drug use, it is also clear that many cultures view substances as an integral part of social bonding and celebration. In some countries, drugs and alcohol are used to enhance the experience of music festivals, parties, and other gatherings. While this can be concerning from a public health perspective, it also underscores the complex and nuanced role that substances play in different cultural contexts. During my travels across America, I have noticed that some places feel like night and day when it comes to homelessness, drug addiction, and public intoxication. I have visited several cities multiple times, and some have left a lasting impression on me, both good and bad. Take New York City, for example—this is the place I want to retire in. There's just something about its fast-paced energy, cultural diversity, and endless opportunities that make it stand out. However, even in a city as incredible as New York, the homelessness crisis is impossible to ignore. Having volunteered at homeless shelters and drug treatment centers, I've seen firsthand how the issue is deeply rooted in addiction, mental health struggles, and systemic failures.

New York isn't alone in this crisis. Places like California, Utah, Seattle, Indianapolis, and, in my opinion, the worst of them all—Philadelphia—are rich in history but are being overrun by homelessness and drug addiction. Walking through some areas of Philadelphia is like walking through a zombie apocalypse. People are strung out on opioids, hunched over in the middle of the sidewalk, and barely functioning. It's heartbreaking to witness, especially knowing that many of these individuals don't have access to proper treatment or support systems. The opioid crisis has hit these cities hard, and it's evident that whatever efforts are in place aren't enough.

Then, on the other hand, you have cities like Miami, New Orleans, Las Vegas, and Memphis, where the issue isn't necessarily drug addiction but rather rampant public intoxication. These cities are known for their nightlife and party culture, and while that attracts tourists, it also creates an environment where excessive drinking is the norm. Walking down Bourbon Street in New Orleans or the Las Vegas Strip, you'll see people stumbling, vomiting on the streets, and passing out on sidewalks. The open-container laws in these cities make it easy for people to drink all day, and many do just that. It's shocking to see so many people willingly putting themselves in dangerous situations simply because the law allows it.

I've been to places where public intoxication is such a common sight that it's almost accepted as normal. In Miami, you can't walk down Ocean Drive without seeing people carrying oversized margaritas at all hours of the day. Memphis, with its deep musical roots and Beale Street's iconic bars, also has an anything-goes drinking culture. These cities may not have the same drug-addiction crisis as places like Philadelphia, but they have their own struggles when it comes to substance abuse. It makes me wonder why alcohol—one of the most damaging substances—is so widely accepted while other drugs are criminalized so harshly.

Not every place I've visited has been this way, though. Some cities have managed to maintain a level of cleanliness and order that I truly respect. Boston, for example, stood out to me as one of the cleanest cities I've been to. The streets were well-maintained, and there was little to no public smoking or obvious signs of drug use. It was refreshing to be in a place where I didn't feel like I had to step over needles or be on high alert for erratic behavior.

Phoenix was another city that impressed me. Despite its growing population, it felt calm and organized. There was very little public smoking, and the streets weren't filled with intoxicated people causing disturbances. I appreciated being able to walk around freely without worrying about stepping into a chaotic environment. The same can be said for Oklahoma City. While it may not be as bustling as New York or as lively as

Miami, it had a sense of order and safety that I found comforting.

Toronto, though technically not in the U.S., also left a great impression on me. Canada as a whole seems to have a different approach to handling homelessness and drug addiction. While I'm sure there are issues, I didn't see them as openly displayed as I did in American cities. Toronto felt organized, and I didn't encounter people smoking on the streets or openly using drugs. It made me wonder what Canada is doing differently to maintain that level of control over these issues.

That's not to say I didn't enjoy myself in cities like New York, Miami, or Las Vegas. Each place has its charm and unique qualities that make it special. But I can't ignore the drastic differences in how different cities handle addiction, homelessness, and public intoxication. Some places seem to have accepted the chaos, while others have taken stricter measures to keep their streets clean and safe.

One thing that continues to shock me is the lack of urgency in addressing these problems in cities that desperately need it. In places like Philadelphia and San Francisco, I saw people living in conditions that no human being should have to endure. Tents lined the sidewalks, people were nodding off in broad daylight, and the streets smelled of urine. It's impossible to walk through these areas and not feel a deep sense of sadness.

At the same time, I've noticed that in cities where public intoxication is a bigger issue, there's almost a celebratory attitude toward it. People travel to Las Vegas, New Orleans, and Miami with the sole purpose of drinking to excess, and it's all fun and games until someone gets hurt. I've witnessed countless people being carried away by their friends, unable to walk or even speak coherently. It's almost as if binge drinking is seen as an acceptable form of self-destruction, while drug addiction is viewed as a moral failing.

There's a clear difference in how cities choose to handle substance abuse. Some places turn a blind eye, letting the problem fester until it becomes impossible to ignore. Others take proactive steps to ensure that their streets remain clean and safe. But what's most concerning is the lack of consistency across the country. The fact that some cities are drowning in addiction and homelessness while others seem to have it under control shows that this isn't just an inevitable consequence of urban life—it's a policy failure. I believe that if cities like Boston, Phoenix, and Toronto can maintain order and limit public substance abuse, then there's no excuse for places like Philadelphia and San Francisco to be in the state they're in. The question is, what are those cities doing differently? Are they investing more in social services? Are they enforcing stricter laws? Are their drug treatment programs more effective?

As someone who has spent time volunteering in shelters and treatment centers, I've seen how difficult it is for people to get the help they need. Many of these individuals don't want to be homeless or addicted, but the system is designed to make it nearly impossible for them to recover. Affordable housing is scarce, mental health services are underfunded, and rehabilitation programs often have long waitlists.

It's frustrating to see how little progress has been made in some cities. In places like Philadelphia, the crisis only seems to be getting worse. Meanwhile, in cities like Boston, things feel much more controlled. The contrast is stark, and it raises important questions about what works and what doesn't when it comes to tackling these issues.

At the end of the day, my travels have given me a new perspective on how America handles addiction and homelessness. I've seen the worst of it, but I've also seen places that give me hope. If one city can figure out a way to maintain order while still offering help to those in need, then every city should be able to do the same. The real challenge is getting leaders to take the issue seriously and implement real, lasting solutions.

Drug laws in the United States are often criticized for their harsh penalties, but compared to many other countries, they are relatively lenient. Nations across Central America, South America, and Southeast Asia enforce strict drug policies, with some imposing life sentences or even the death penalty for possession or trafficking. Countries such as Malaysia, Indonesia, and Singapore maintain a zero-tolerance approach, automatically assuming that those caught with even small amounts of drugs are dealers. In places like Vietnam and Saudi Arabia, individuals convicted of drug crimes may face execution, showing how seriously these governments take the issue.

Despite never having visited any of these countries, I have a strong interest in learning about their legal systems and how they sustain such rigid laws. Many of these nations have a history of drug-related issues, which has likely shaped their severe policies. For example, Iran struggles with opium addiction due to its proximity to Afghanistan, a major producer of the drug. Thailand and the Philippines have both waged aggressive wars on drugs, leading to thousands of arrests and executions. Understanding the cultural, historical, and political factors behind these strict regulations would provide valuable insight into how different societies combat drug-related crime.

One of the most fascinating aspects of these legal systems is the way they combine law enforcement with rehabilitation. Some countries, like China and Thailand, mandate government-run rehab programs for those caught with drugs, while others, like Cambodia and Colombia, rely on incarceration as the primary punishment. In Dubai, even failing a drug test—

without possessing any drugs—can result in imprisonment and deportation. These policies reflect broader attitudes toward crime and punishment, raising important questions about effectiveness, human rights, and the long-term impact on individuals and communities.

Visiting these countries is high on my list of future travel plans because I want to witness firsthand how they enforce these laws and what their impact is on society. Exploring these regions would allow me to engage with locals, legal experts, and activists to understand both the benefits and drawbacks of such strict policies. Additionally, seeing how these governments balance law enforcement, rehabilitation, and prevention strategies could provide valuable lessons for addressing drug-related issues in the United States. The global fight against drug abuse is complex, and each country's approach offers a unique perspective on how to tackle this ongoing crisis.

Similar to Prophet Muhammad's purification by Angel Jibril, my travels have cleansed my heart, allowing me to empathize deeply with those struggling. This journey has become a spiritual odyssey, refined my purpose, and equip me with tools to support others. Through trials and triumphs, Allah has purified my heart, enabling me to serve my community.

CHAPTER 3

NO END IN SIGHT

THE NIXON ADMINISTRATION

"America's public enemy number one in the United States is drug abuse. In order to fight and defeat this enemy, it is necessary to wage a new, all-out offensive."
— Richard Nixon

In 1971, President Richard Nixon declared drug abuse to be "public enemy number one," launching what would become the War on Drugs—a decades-long campaign aimed at eliminating illegal drug use and trafficking in the United States. While Nixon's policies initially focused on rehabilitation and treatment, they later shifted toward law enforcement and punishment, setting the stage for mass incarceration and racial disparities in drug policy enforcement.

The creation of the Drug Enforcement Administration (DEA) in 1973 further institutionalized this war, leading to aggressive policing tactics and punitive drug laws. Though Nixon's war on drugs was framed as a fight to protect public health and safety, evidence suggests that political and racial motivations played a major role in shaping its enforcement.

The late 1960s and early 1970s saw a significant rise in drug use, particularly among hippie counterculture groups, anti-war protesters, and Vietnam War veterans. Marijuana, LSD, and heroin became especially prevalent, sparking national concern about the growing drug epidemic. Against this backdrop, Nixon addressed Congress in 1971, calling drug abuse "public enemy number one" and proposing stronger federal action to combat addiction and illegal drug distribution. This marked the official beginning of the War on Drugs, shifting U.S. policy toward greater federal involvement in drug control.

Nixon's rhetoric painted drug use as both a moral failure and a national security threat, linking it to urban crime and social unrest. His administration emphasized that reducing drug abuse was essential to restoring law and order, a key campaign promise that resonated with many conservative voters. However, while Nixon framed the war as a means to combat crime, his approach to enforcement and punishment disproportionately impacted marginalized communities, setting a precedent for future administrations.

One of Nixon's most lasting contributions to drug policy was the Controlled Substances Act (CSA) of 1970. This law established a system of drug scheduling, classifying substances into five categories based on their medical use and potential for abuse. Schedule I drugs, such as heroin, LSD, and marijuana, were deemed to have no medical value and were subjected to the strictest regulations. Meanwhile, drugs like cocaine and methamphetamine were placed in lower schedules despite their addictive properties.

The CSA laid the foundation for future drug enforcement policies, giving federal agencies the authority to criminalize certain substances and prosecute those who manufactured or distributed them. Critics argue that the classification system was based more on political motivations than scientific evidence, particularly in the case of marijuana, which was heavily criminalized despite ongoing debates over its medicinal value.

Unlike later administrations, Nixon's War on Drugs initially included a public health approach alongside criminal enforcement. In 1971, he dramatically increased federal funding for drug treatment programs, recognizing that addiction was a disease rather than just a crime. Programs such as methadone clinics for heroin addicts received substantial support, and the government invested in research on addiction prevention.

Additionally, Nixon established the Special Action Office for Drug Abuse Prevention (SAODAP), which prioritized rehabilitation efforts over incarceration. This was a significant departure from the punitive drug policies that would dominate the 1980s and 1990s. However, despite these early efforts, Nixon's administration eventually pivoted toward a more aggressive law enforcement strategy, which would shape the War on Drugs for decades to come.

By 1973, Nixon's War on Drugs had shifted away from rehabilitation and toward increased policing, surveillance, and international drug interdiction efforts. That year, he created the Drug Enforcement Administration (DEA), consolidating several federal agencies to intensify drug enforcement efforts. The DEA was granted broad authority to conduct drug raids, seize assets, and arrest those involved in drug trafficking.

To launch his anti-drug campaign, Nixon allocated unprecedented federal funding to drug enforcement agencies and treatment programs. In 1971, he requested $155 million (equivalent to nearly $1 billion today) to fund the War on

Drugs. By 1973, he had increased the budget to $600 million (around $4 billion today). The money was primarily used for: Expanding law enforcement agencies, including the newly established Drug Enforcement Administration (DEA) in 1973, Increasing border security to stop drug trafficking, Funding rehabilitation programs and drug treatment centers (though these efforts were later reduced under future administrations) and Launching anti-drug propaganda campaigns.

The DEA's creation marked a turning point in federal drug policy, as the focus moved away from treating addiction and toward punishing users and dealers. Nixon's administration also launched Operation Intercept, a controversial initiative that aimed to curb the flow of drugs from Mexico by imposing strict border inspections. The program was largely unsuccessful and caused major disruptions to the economy, but it reinforced the idea that drug enforcement required militarized tactics and border crackdowns.

Although Nixon publicly framed the War on Drugs as a necessary battle against addiction and crime, evidence suggests that political and racial motivations played a significant role in its implementation. In a 1994 interview, Nixon's former domestic policy advisor, John Ehrlichman, admitted that the War on Drugs was strategically designed to target Black communities and anti-war activists. Ehrlichman stated:

"We knew we couldn't make it illegal to be either against the war or Black, but by getting the public to associate the hippies with marijuana and Blacks with heroin, and then criminalizing both heavily, we could disrupt those communities."

This confession underscores how Nixon's policies were used

as tools for political repression, disproportionately affecting communities of color. Although drug use was prevalent across racial lines, enforcement was heavily concentrated in Black and Latino neighborhoods, leading to mass arrests and long-term economic and social damage.

While Nixon's War on Drugs did not create mass incarceration on its own, it laid the foundation for the explosion of the U.S. prison population in the 1980s and 1990s. His administration's emphasis on law enforcement and mandatory sentencing contributed to the disproportionate incarceration of Black and Latino individuals.

Nixon's policies introduced the idea that drug use should be punished through harsh criminal sentences rather than treated as a public health issue. This mindset persisted through later administrations, culminating in the 1980s mandatory minimum sentencing laws under Ronald Reagan and the 1994 Crime Bill under Bill Clinton, both of which fueled mass incarceration.

Richard Nixon's War on Drugs was a pivotal moment in U.S. history that reshaped the nation's approach to drug policy, law enforcement, and criminal justice. While Nixon initially pursued a public health strategy, his administration ultimately prioritized criminalization and enforcement, leading to the creation of the DEA and the expansion of drug-related policing. The racial and political motivations behind the War on Drugs resulted in systemic injustices, disproportionately targeting Black communities and setting the stage for the mass incarceration crisis that followed in later decades.

Though the War on Drugs was intended to combat addiction and crime, its consequences have been far-reaching, leading to decades of punitive policies, racial disparities, and a broken criminal justice system. Speaking of decades later, President Ronald Regan and First Lady Nancy Regan made it a mission and priority to combat the war on drugs during the Regan administration.

THE REGAN ADMINISTRATION

Unlike the 70's, in the early 1980s, the United States found itself grappling with what was portrayed as a growing drug epidemic, particularly the surge in crack cocaine use in urban areas. The Reagan administration's response to this crisis was the declaration of a "War on Drugs," a broad initiative aimed at reducing drug use and combating drug-related crime. While the "War on Drugs" was a response to genuine concerns about public safety, its policies were heavily criticized for their overemphasis on law enforcement and punitive measures. At the same time, First Lady Nancy Reagan launched her "Just Say No" campaign, a well-intentioned initiative aimed at preventing youth drug use. Both of these efforts had far-reaching consequences, particularly for communities of color, and their legacy continues to shape America's approach to drug policy.

The "War on Drugs" officially began in 1985 when the Reagan administration escalated efforts to combat drug use and trafficking. The surge in drug use, particularly crack cocaine, which was seen as more addictive and widely available, spurred panic among many Americans. Reagan's campaign was, in part, a response to public concern over the rise in violent crime often associated with drug trafficking. The administration's approach framed drug addiction as a moral failing rather than a public health issue, which would set the tone for future policies. Reagan's rhetoric emphasized that drugs were an existential threat to American society, urging a militarized response that would involve the DEA, local law enforcement, and military intervention.

At the heart of the "War on Drugs" was a tough-on-crime agenda, embodied by policies that prioritized law enforcement over prevention and treatment. The Anti-Drug Abuse Act of 1986, one of the cornerstones of this initiative, introduced mandatory minimum sentences for drug offenders, which would lead to the mass incarceration of drug users and small-time offenders.

This law also created harsher penalties for crack cocaine offenses, which were more prevalent in poorer urban areas, compared to powder cocaine, which was typically associated with wealthier, predominantly white communities. The disparities in sentencing between crack and powder cocaine would become a significant point of contention and a source of criticism for the policies that followed.

While the "War on Drugs" sought to curb the supply of illicit substances, the "Just Say No" campaign, launched by Nancy Reagan in 1985, focused on prevention. Aimed primarily at children and teenagers, the campaign relied on the simplistic message that the best way to avoid the dangers of drug use was to simply refuse. Using public service announcements, school programs, and celebrity endorsements, the campaign emphasized personal responsibility and the power of saying "no" to drugs. The initiative was positioned as an antidote to the growing influence of drug culture, and its impact was felt nationwide, with schools hosting rallies, celebrities speaking out, and the message echoing throughout American culture.

The "Just Say No" campaign was part of a broader cultural effort to combat drug use, but its effectiveness remains highly debated. While the message of personal responsibility resonated with many, critics argued that it oversimplified the issue of drug addiction. Addiction is a complex, multifaceted problem that cannot simply be solved by telling people to say "no." Furthermore, the campaign did little to address the root causes of drug use, such as poverty, lack of access to education, and social inequality. The campaign's failure to offer a deeper understanding of drug addiction was one of the key criticisms leveled against it.

The financial commitment to the "War on Drugs" and Nancy Reagan's "Just Say No" campaign was significant, with millions of dollars allocated to fund the initiatives. During the Reagan administration, the federal government spent substantial amounts to support anti-drug programs, law enforcement, and public awareness efforts. By 1989, the United States government had allocated over $2 billion to combat drug use and trafficking, and the funding increased in subsequent years. This included money for law enforcement operations, drug interdiction programs, and expanding the infrastructure for the Drug Enforcement Administration (DEA) to enhance its ability to target drug cartels.

One of the major sources of funding for anti-drug initiatives came from the public and private sectors, with the Reagan administration encouraging donations to various anti-drug causes. The government also sought support from the private sector to fund awareness campaigns, including the "Just Say No" initiative. The campaign itself was largely funded through private donations and corporate sponsorships, and by 1986, the "Just Say No" Foundation had raised over $8 million to support its programs, which included educational materials, media campaigns, and the organization of events. This funding was crucial in sustaining the campaign's visibility and impact in schools and communities across the United States.

Despite the significant amount of money raised for prevention and enforcement, critics have argued that the funds could have been more effectively allocated. A large portion of the budget for the "War on Drugs" was directed toward expanding the criminal justice system—particularly through increased funding for law enforcement, prisons, and the militarization of police forces—rather than for treatment or rehabilitation programs. In contrast, the "Just Say No" campaign, while popular and highly visible, struggled to show measurable success in curbing drug use, leading some to question the effectiveness of its funding. The lack of a significant shift in drug use statistics despite the substantial financial commitment led to criticisms that the focus on enforcement rather than treatment was misguided.

On the other hand, private and corporate donors played an essential role in supporting the "Just Say No" campaign. Major companies, including McDonald's, Burger King, and Coca-Cola, contributed millions to the initiative. These corporate donations helped fuel a high-profile media campaign, including commercials, advertisements, and school-based programs. Yet, while the corporate involvement gave the campaign a level of national prominence, it also raised concerns about the commercialization of anti-drug messages and the simplicity of the message being promoted.

Furthermore, while the "War on Drugs" saw substantial funding directed toward punitive measures, much of the financial burden ultimately fell on state and local governments, which were responsible for carrying out many of the policies enacted at the federal level. The costs associated with law enforcement, incarceration, and the construction of new prisons resulted in a massive strain on public resources. By the end of the 1980s and into the 1990s, state governments were grappling with the financial burden of maintaining a rapidly growing prison population, which would continue to escalate through the 1990s.

In addition to the shortcomings of the "Just Say No" campaign, the "War on Drugs" policies led to far-reaching consequences, particularly for minority communities. African Americans and Latinos were disproportionately affected by the policies enacted during the 1980s. Despite studies showing that drug use was roughly equivalent across racial lines, the enforcement of drug laws targeted minority populations at a far higher rate. The crack cocaine sentencing disparities, where crack cocaine offenses carried far harsher sentences than powder cocaine offenses, became a symbol of racial inequity in the justice system. Communities of color were systematically over-policed and over-incarcerated, contributing to the cycle of poverty and disenfranchisement.

The mass incarceration of African Americans and Latinos was perhaps the most destructive outcome of the "War on Drugs." As the prison population swelled, many individuals were incarcerated for low-level drug offenses, with little opportunity for rehabilitation. The focus on punitive measures rather than treatment or rehabilitation further entrenched social and racial inequalities. This period marked the beginning of what would later be called the "mass incarceration" era, which saw the United States develop the highest incarceration rate in the world.

The impact of the "War on Drugs" on the American population was not only seen in the financial expenditures but also in the significant number of arrests and deaths associated with drug use and law enforcement actions. The "War on Drugs" led to a dramatic increase in arrests, particularly among African American and Latino communities. By the mid-1990s, nearly half of all drug arrests were for possession of marijuana, despite the fact that marijuana use was similar across racial groups.

However, the racial disparity in arrests became even more evident in the enforcement of laws related to crack cocaine. African Americans were disproportionately arrested for crack-related offenses, and they received much harsher sentences than white individuals charged with powder cocaine offenses, even though the two drugs are chemically similar.

In 1980, there were a lot of people incarcerated for drug-related offenses. By 1997, that number had skyrocketed to more than one could imagine. Reflecting the enormous increase in arrests and imprisonment under the "War on Drugs." This surge in incarceration came alongside a broader rise in arrests for nonviolent offenses, often resulting in lengthy prison sentences that contributed to the mass incarceration of marginalized communities. The disproportionate focus on arresting low-level drug offenders further strained the criminal justice system and led to overcrowded prisons that struggled to accommodate the growing number of incarcerated individuals.

Moreover, the "War on Drugs" exacerbated the problem of racial profiling and policing in urban areas. The increased police presence in poor, predominantly minority neighborhoods, coupled with aggressive tactics such as stop-and-frisk policies, led to a dramatic rise in encounters between law enforcement and civilians. These interactions often resulted in violent confrontations, with officers using excessive force against drug suspects. The death toll linked to drug-related violence and law enforcement actions during the 1980s and 1990s reflected the brutal nature of the "War on Drugs." In cities like New York, Los Angeles, and Chicago, drug-related shootings and standoffs between drug dealers and police became a regular part of the urban landscape.

The rise in arrests also correlated with an increase in deaths associated with drug use, both directly and indirectly. The 1980s saw an alarming increase in the death rate from crack cocaine overdose. Although the epidemic was primarily centered in urban areas, it quickly spread to suburban regions. According to the Centers for Disease Control and Prevention, between 1982 and 1989, the number of drug overdose deaths tripled, largely due to the widespread use of crack cocaine. The intense media coverage of crack-related deaths, particularly in impoverished communities, fueled the panic that justified the harsh anti-drug policies of the time.

Additionally, the Reagan-era drug policies led to the criminalization of drug addiction itself. Instead of focusing on rehabilitation and treatment programs, drug users were often treated as criminals and sent to prison. This approach not only failed to reduce addiction but also led to higher death rates as individuals, once incarcerated, faced difficult and dangerous conditions in prisons. The overcrowded prison systems failed to provide adequate healthcare or treatment for those suffering from addiction, exacerbating the underlying issue of drug dependency. This set the stage for a public health crisis that would continue well into the next decades.

As the "War on Drugs" progressed, the toll on communities continued to mount. While public officials praised the success of the initiative in reducing drug availability, many urban areas continued to experience high levels of violence and death related to drugs. The rise in gang violence, fueled by the competition over drug sales, added another layer of tragedy. The high body count and societal damage caused by the Reagan-era policies would become an indelible mark on the national consciousness, with many later questioning whether the War on Drugs was truly effective in addressing the underlying issues of addiction and poverty.

The "War on Drugs" and the "Just Say No" campaign, despite their efforts, contributed to a cycle of criminalization that disproportionately affected minority communities, while also failing to reduce drug use in any significant manner. The massive increase in arrests and the mounting death toll, particularly from overdose and violence, became central to the critiques of these policies. The American public's growing awareness of the devastating effects of the "War on Drugs" set the stage for eventual reforms in drug policy that would follow in the years to come, including a reevaluation of the criminal justice system and a shift toward more treatment-focused approaches to drug addiction.

The backlash against the "War on Drugs" and the "Just Say No" campaign began to mount as the decade progressed. Activists and civil rights organizations criticized the racial disparities in drug law enforcement and the over-reliance on incarceration. The public began to question the effectiveness of a drug policy that prioritized punishment over prevention or rehabilitation. While the Reagan administration remained steadfast in its position, the criticisms of the policies were hard to ignore. By the end of the 1980s, many were calling for a shift in how America approached drug use, focusing on treatment rather than criminalization.

Despite the criticism, the Reagan administration's policies persisted, and the momentum continued into the 1990s. However, as the 1990s approached, there was a growing recognition that the "War on Drugs" was not succeeding in reducing drug use or crime. There was a shift in public opinion, with an increasing number of voices calling for drug policy reform. The growing acknowledgment of the failure of the "War on Drugs" would set the stage for new approaches to drug law enforcement in the coming decades.

While the "War on Drugs" was largely seen as a failure, its impact on American society was undeniable. The policies put in place during the 1980s laid the groundwork for a new criminal justice reality, where drug offenses were treated with extreme severity. These policies also set the stage for the continuing stigmatization of drug users, who were viewed primarily as criminals rather than individuals in need of help.

Furthermore, the enduring focus on criminal justice responses to drug use would shape the national conversation about addiction for decades to come.

By the time of Bill Clinton's presidency in the 1990s, it was clear that the "War on Drugs" had failed to achieve its intended results. Drug addiction and drug-related crime had not decreased, and the racial disparities in the criminal justice system were becoming more pronounced. Yet, rather than significantly shifting toward a public health-oriented approach, the Clinton administration passed the Violent Crime Control and Law Enforcement Act of 1994, which expanded on the policies of the Reagan era. The 1994 crime bill, which included provisions for more prison construction and the expansion of the death penalty, further entrenched the "tough on crime" approach that had defined the previous decades.

The 1994 crime bill marked a continuation of the "War on Drugs" policies, but it also reflected the increasing recognition of the need to address crime in a more comprehensive way. Although the bill included some provisions for drug treatment programs, it was still heavily focused on law enforcement and incarceration. The legacy of the Reagan-era drug policies, coupled with the Clinton administration's continuation of those policies, set the stage for the next phase in America's ongoing struggle with drug addiction, crime, and mass incarceration.

THE CLINTON ADMINISTRATION

The 1994 Violent Crime Control and Law Enforcement Act, also known as the 1994 Crime Bill, was a landmark piece of legislation signed into law by President Bill Clinton. At the time, the bill was presented as a comprehensive solution to rising crime rates in the U.S. during the 1980s and early 1990s. While it included a wide range of measures aimed at reducing violent crime, it also played a significant role in expanding the scope of the "War on Drugs" initiated in the 1980s. The bill's provisions had a profound effect on law enforcement practices, drug-related crime, and the criminal justice system in the United States, which led to both praise and criticism over the years.

One of the major components of the 1994 Crime Bill was its emphasis on increasing federal support for law enforcement agencies. The bill allocated $30 billion in federal funding to hire additional police officers, build new prisons, and implement community policing initiatives. The idea behind this provision was to increase the presence of law enforcement in high-crime areas, particularly urban neighborhoods that had been devastated by the crack cocaine epidemic. These measures, while intended to lower crime rates, also had unintended consequences, including the militarization of police forces and a rise in aggressive policing tactics, especially in marginalized communities.

The Crime Bill also included the "three strikes" rule, which mandated life sentences without parole for individuals convicted of three or more serious felonies. This provision targeted repeat offenders, particularly those involved in violent crimes and drug-related offenses. While it was hailed as a tough-on-crime measure, it disproportionately impacted those involved in nonviolent crimes, including drug offenses. This contributed to the significant increase in the U.S. prison population, leading to what is now known as mass incarceration. By 2000, the U.S. prison population had ballooned to over 2 million, a trend that the Crime Bill helped accelerate.

Another critical aspect of the bill was the expansion of the death penalty for certain federal crimes, including drug trafficking. The bill allowed for the death penalty to be applied to individuals convicted of major drug offenses, including those involved in the distribution of drugs like crack cocaine. This provision was seen as a continuation of the punitive approach to drug policy that had gained momentum during the Reagan and Bush administrations. While supporters of the bill argued that it was necessary to crack down on drug cartels, critics pointed out that it would likely lead to a disproportionate number of executions for people of color, further exacerbating racial disparities in the criminal justice system.

The 1994 Crime Bill's impact on drug laws was particularly notable in its continuation of policies from the previous decades. The bill reinforced existing laws, including the mandatory minimum sentencing for certain drug offenses. One of the most controversial provisions of the Crime Bill was its continuation of the crack versus powder cocaine sentencing disparity, which imposed far harsher sentences for crack cocaine offenses, typically committed by African Americans, than for powder cocaine offenses, which were more commonly associated with white users. This sentencing disparity fueled widespread criticism of the bill, as it disproportionately affected black and Latino communities, further perpetuating racial inequality in the criminal justice system.

The Clinton administration's approach to drugs, encapsulated in the 1994 Crime Bill, marked a shift toward a more punitive model, focusing on law enforcement and incarceration rather than public health and rehabilitation. While the bill included some provisions for prevention and treatment, the vast majority of the resources were directed toward law enforcement and criminal penalties. Critics argued that this approach failed to address the root causes of drug addiction and instead criminalized individuals, particularly in inner-city communities, without offering sufficient opportunities for recovery or rehabilitation. The bill's emphasis on punishment over treatment led to an increase in the number of people incarcerated for nonviolent drug offenses.

In terms of the financial impact, the Crime Bill's emphasis on expanding the prison system and funding law enforcement meant significant federal, state, and local government expenditures. The bill funded the construction of thousands of new prison beds, adding to the burgeoning U.S. prison population. However, the financial burden of incarcerating so many individuals soon became apparent. Local and state governments, faced with increasing prison populations, were forced to allocate more and more of their budgets to maintaining prisons, diverting funds from education, healthcare, and other social services. In many ways, the financial costs of the Crime Bill continue to be felt, particularly in economically disadvantaged communities where the effects of mass incarceration have led to deep social and economic scars.

As a direct result of the 1994 Crime Bill, the U.S. prison population grew at an unprecedented rate. The number of people incarcerated in the U.S. more than doubled from approximately 1.2 million in 1990 to over 2 million by the early 2000s. While this increase in incarceration was framed as a success in reducing crime rates, the reality was far more complex. Studies have shown that the growth in the prison population was not directly tied to a reduction in crime, but rather to changes in sentencing laws, the over-policing of certain communities, and the criminalization of drug use. As a result, the U.S. became the world leader in incarceration, a distinction that brought with it significant social and economic consequences.

The racial disparities in arrests, convictions, and sentencing also became a central issue in discussions about the Crime Bill's impact. African Americans, despite using and selling drugs at similar rates to white Americans, were disproportionately arrested and incarcerated for drug offenses. The mandatory minimum sentences for crack cocaine, in particular, led to the overrepresentation of black men in U.S. prisons. Studies from organizations like the NAACP and The Sentencing Project highlighted the racially biased nature of drug enforcement, which exacerbated existing racial inequalities in the justice system. The Crime Bill, while not explicitly targeting any one race, reinforced these inequalities by continuing the policies that disproportionately impacted communities of color.

In addition to its racial implications, the Crime Bill led to a public health crisis by prioritizing punitive measures over harm reduction or rehabilitation. Drug addiction was increasingly viewed as a criminal issue rather than a public health issue. As a result, individuals struggling with addiction were incarcerated rather than provided with access to treatment programs. The limited funding for drug treatment programs in the Crime Bill was overshadowed by the billions directed at prisons and law enforcement, leaving many drug users without the help they needed to recover. The criminalization of addiction had long-lasting effects on individuals and communities, many of whom were left without the resources to address the root causes of drug dependency.

In response to the Crime Bill's consequences, several reform movements emerged in the late 1990s and early 2000s. Advocates for criminal justice reform, including civil rights organizations and drug policy experts, began calling for a reevaluation of the nation's approach to drugs and crime. They pointed to the racial disparities in arrests, the over-incarceration of nonviolent offenders, and the failure of punitive drug policies to reduce addiction or crime. In the years following the passage of the Crime Bill, these voices grew louder, culminating in a national conversation about the need for criminal justice reform and the rethinking of the U.S. approach to drug policy.

One of the most significant reforms that came about in response to the Crime Bill was the Fair Sentencing Act of 2010, which sought to address the crack-cocaine sentencing disparity that had been a key component of the 1994 Crime Bill. The Fair Sentencing Act reduced the disparity between the sentencing of crack and powder cocaine, though it did not eliminate it entirely. This reform was seen as a step toward rectifying some of the damage done by the 1994 Crime Bill, but advocates argue that more work is needed to address the systemic issues of racial inequality and mass incarceration.

Another important reform came with the passage of the First Step Act in 2018, which aimed to reduce sentences for nonviolent drug offenders and provided increased opportunities for rehabilitation. While it did not undo the damage caused by the 1994 Crime Bill, it marked a significant shift in U.S. criminal justice policy, as lawmakers began to recognize the flaws in the tough-on-crime approach that had dominated for decades. The Act also sought to address racial disparities in sentencing, further highlighting the growing recognition that criminal justice reform was necessary to create a more equitable system.

In 1970 there was about 415,000 drug related arrests taken place from this the prison population was around 200,000 from drugs. Unfortunately, the next decade we see these numbers increase going to 580,900 drug related arrest and over 500,000 people populated the prison from drug related crimes. Wait there is more, the following decade it get worst. There was roughly 1,089,500 drug related arrests and over 1,150,000 people populating the prison systems. These number is to illustrates the dramatic increase in drug-related arrests and prison populations due to Nixon's policies and their continuation under later administrations.

The War on Drugs extended beyond the U.S., influencing policies worldwide. Several countries started to follow America's lead, implementing stricter drug laws and increasing penalties for drug offenses. However, the results were often catastrophic.

Over 50 million people worldwide were arrested for drug-related offenses, More than 2 million deaths were linked to drug overdoses, violence, and harsh criminal sentences, Thousands of families were separated due to long prison sentences, Countries like Colombia and Mexico experienced extreme violence due to drug cartel wars, fueled by the illegal drug trade.

One of the biggest failures of the War on Drugs was its inability to prevent overdose deaths. Instead of reducing drug use, prohibition drove the drug trade underground, making it even more dangerous.

In the America overdose death grew significantly larger year by year from 1970 to the year 2000. For example, in 1970 overdose death was around 6,100 in America. Literally ten years later we see a major spike in overdose death because the death rate reached 12,900 people. At this rate you would think that America would have pivot its agenda to slowing down overdose deaths. In 1990 there was about 19,300 recorded overdose in America which is less than the year 2000 which saw 26,200 overdose. This data highlights the failure of the War on Drugs to prevent fatalities, as overdose deaths continued to rise despite strict drug laws.

THE PRESENT ERA ADMINISTRATION

The War on Drugs in the present time has evolved significantly from its origins in the 1970s and 1980s, but its impact continues to shape American society. While past administrations focused on criminalization and aggressive enforcement, recent years have seen a shift toward decriminalization, rehabilitation, and policy reform. Despite some progress, racial disparities, mass incarceration, and the opioid epidemic still present significant challenges. The focus of today's drug policies is increasingly centered on criminal justice reform, marijuana legalization, the public health response to addiction, and addressing the ongoing racial inequities created by decades of punitive measures.

One of the most notable changes in the War on Drugs today is the movement toward criminal justice reform. After decades of strict drug laws that disproportionately affected communities of color, there has been growing bipartisan support for policy changes that reduce harsh sentencing for nonviolent drug offenses. The First Step Act of 2018, for example, was a significant federal effort to reform sentencing laws, expand rehabilitation programs in prisons, and allow for the early release of certain low-risk offenders. This law was particularly important in addressing the excessive sentences handed down during the crack cocaine epidemic of the 1980s and 1990s.

In addition to federal reforms, state-level policies have played a major role in reshaping drug enforcement. Several states have passed laws reducing or eliminating mandatory minimum sentences for drug offenses, and some have established diversion programs that allow nonviolent drug offenders to receive treatment instead of serving time in prison. These changes reflect a growing recognition that long prison sentences for drug-related offenses do little to address addiction and often contribute to cycles of poverty and recidivism.

Another major development in the modern War on Drugs is the legalization and decriminalization of marijuana. Over the past decade, a growing number of states have legalized marijuana for both medical and recreational use. As of 2024, more than 20 states have fully legalized recreational marijuana, while many others have decriminalized possession. This shift represents a significant departure from past drug policies, which often resulted in harsh punishments for even minor marijuana offenses.

The economic impact of marijuana legalization has also been substantial. States that have legalized cannabis have generated billions of dollars in tax revenue, much of which has been allocated to public education, healthcare, and social programs. Additionally, the legal cannabis industry has created thousands of jobs, providing economic opportunities in both urban and rural areas. However, despite these benefits, challenges remain, particularly regarding federal prohibition, which continues to create conflicts between state and federal law.

While legalization has reduced arrests for marijuana offenses, many individuals, particularly people of color, still face the long-term consequences of past drug convictions. Even in states where marijuana is now legal, individuals with prior convictions often struggle to find employment, secure housing, or regain voting rights. Some states have implemented expungement programs to clear the records of those with nonviolent marijuana-related offenses, but the process is often slow and bureaucratic, leaving many affected individuals without relief.

Beyond marijuana policy, the opioid crisis has dramatically reshaped how drug addiction is addressed in the United States. Unlike previous drug epidemics, which were primarily met with punitive law enforcement responses, the opioid crisis has been increasingly treated as a public health emergency. This shift in approach has led to expanded access to addiction treatment, harm reduction programs, and greater scrutiny of pharmaceutical companies that contributed to the crisis through the over-prescription of opioids.

One of the most effective strategies in combating opioid overdoses has been the distribution of naloxone, a life-saving medication that can reverse opioid overdoses. Many states have passed laws making naloxone more accessible, and some police departments and first responders now carry it as part of their standard medical supplies. Additionally, harm reduction programs, such as needle exchange initiatives, have been implemented in several states to reduce the spread of infectious diseases among drug users.

Despite these changes, there are still significant racial disparities in how drug addiction is treated. The opioid crisis, which has predominantly affected white communities, has been met with a response focused on treatment and rehabilitation, whereas past drug crises, such as the crack cocaine epidemic of the 1980s and 1990s, were largely met with incarceration and punitive policies. This disparity highlights the racial biases that have long been embedded in drug enforcement policies.

Although the public health response to opioid addiction has been more compassionate, communities of color continue to face harsher penalties for drug-related offenses. Black and Latino Americans are still disproportionately arrested and imprisoned for drug possession, despite similar rates of drug use across racial groups. These disparities indicate that while policies have shifted, systemic issues in law enforcement and the judicial system remain deeply entrenched.

Some states have taken steps to address racial disparities in drug enforcement by implementing policies that provide alternative sentencing for nonviolent drug offenses. For example, some jurisdictions now offer drug courts, which allow individuals to complete treatment programs in exchange for reduced sentences or the dismissal of charges. These initiatives are designed to break the cycle of incarceration and provide individuals with the support they need to overcome addiction.

At the international level, some countries have adopted decriminalization models that the U.S. is beginning to consider. For instance, Portugal decriminalized all drugs in 2001, shifting its focus from punishment to treatment. Since then, the country has seen a significant decline in drug-related deaths and incarceration rates. Some U.S. states, such as Oregon, have experimented with similar policies by decriminalizing small amounts of drugs and redirecting funds from law enforcement to addiction treatment programs.

While decriminalization efforts have gained traction, opposition to these policies remains strong in some parts of the country. Critics argue that decriminalization could lead to increased drug use and pose public safety risks. However, advocates counter that the current approach of criminalization has failed to reduce drug use and has instead fueled mass incarceration and systemic inequality. The debate over how best to address drug addiction continues to be a contentious issue in American politics.

The economic and social consequences of the War on Drugs continue to be felt today. Communities that were heavily impacted by aggressive drug enforcement policies in past decades still experience higher levels of poverty, unemployment, and limited access to education. Many advocates argue that true reform requires not just changes in drug laws, but also investment in communities that have been disproportionately affected by past policies. Programs that provide job training, mental health services, and affordable housing are seen as essential in addressing the root causes of drug addiction and crime.

The United States continues to grapple with an unprecedented drug crisis, primarily fueled by the abuse of prescription and nonprescription opioids. The easy accessibility of these drugs has created a devastating public health emergency, with individuals rapidly transitioning from prescribed medications to illicit substances such as heroin and fentanyl. The rise in opioid dependency has led to an increase in overdoses, hospitalizations, and fatalities, making this crisis one of the most pressing challenges facing American society today.

One of the key factors in the opioid crisis is the widespread abuse of prescription painkillers. Many individuals initially become addicted through legally prescribed medications, only to later seek out illicit alternatives when prescriptions become too expensive or difficult to obtain. This shift from medical use to dependency has been a gateway for heroin use, as heroin is often cheaper and more accessible than prescription opioids.

Synthetic opioids, particularly fentanyl, have played a major role in the rapid rise of overdose deaths in the United States. Fentanyl is estimated to be 40 times more potent than heroin and nearly 100 times more potent than morphine. Many drug users unknowingly consume fentanyl-laced heroin, dramatically increasing the likelihood of overdose. Additionally, fentanyl analogs such as acetyl fentanyl are often trafficked into the U.S., further complicating efforts to curb the epidemic.

Much of the fentanyl entering the U.S. originates from China and Mexico. China has been a significant source of illicitly manufactured fentanyl and its analogs, which are often shipped to Mexico before being smuggled across the U.S. border. The increase in opium poppy cultivation in Mexico has also contributed to a surge in heroin production, with Mexican drug cartels supplying the majority of heroin consumed in the United States.

The trafficking of heroin and other narcotics across the U.S.-Mexico border has intensified in recent years. Between 2010 and 2015, the number of heroin seizures at the border more than doubled. In addition to heroin, Mexican drug cartels are responsible for smuggling large quantities of cocaine, methamphetamine, and marijuana into the United States. These cartels not only control the flow of drugs into the country but also oversee a significant portion of the drug distribution networks operating within the U.S.

Despite efforts by the DEA and other law enforcement agencies, drug trafficking organizations continue to evolve. Smugglers now use encrypted technology and social media platforms to coordinate drug shipments and recruit new members. These advanced techniques make it more difficult for law enforcement to track and dismantle drug networks, allowing cartels to operate with greater efficiency and anonymity.

Recent statistics on drug trafficking highlight the scale of the problem. In 2016, the majority of drug traffickers (84.9%) were male, with an average age of 36. Nearly 70% of all offenders were U.S. citizens, and almost half had little or no prior criminal history. The increasing involvement of individuals with no prior offenses suggests that drug trafficking is becoming more widespread and accessible to a broader demographic.

The DEA has identified Mexican drug cartels as the most dominant players in the U.S. drug trade. The Sinaloa Cartel, Jalisco New Generation Cartel, Juarez Cartel, Gulf Cartel, Los Zetas, and the Beltran-Leyva Organization all have significant influence over drug trafficking operations within the United States. These organizations control vast distribution networks and maintain strong connections with local gangs and street-level dealers.

Drug trafficking offenses in the United States are largely concentrated in specific regions. The Western and Southern Districts of Texas, the District of Arizona, the Southern District of California, and the District of New Mexico are among the top five areas for drug trafficking activity. These locations serve as key entry points for drugs smuggled across the U.S.-Mexico border.

Methamphetamine, cocaine, marijuana, heroin, crack cocaine, and oxycodone account for nearly all drug trafficking offenses. In 2016, methamphetamine was the most commonly trafficked drug, responsible for 33.6% of all trafficking cases. Cocaine accounted for 19.8%, marijuana for 17.6%, heroin for 14.4%, crack for 8.1%, and oxycodone for 2.8%. The prevalence of methamphetamine trafficking underscores the growing demand for synthetic drugs in the U.S.

One of the most dangerous aspects of the current drug crisis is the adulteration of narcotics. When large drug shipments arrive in the U.S., they are often taken to "stash houses" where they are broken down into smaller quantities and mixed with various additives. Common adulterants include sugars, caffeine, quinine, paracetamol, and procaine. In recent years, fentanyl and its analogs have increasingly been used as cutting agents, making street drugs far more lethal.

Adulterated drugs pose a significant threat to public safety because users often have no knowledge of what they are consuming. A heroin user may unknowingly ingest a lethal dose of fentanyl, leading to an overdose. Similarly, counterfeit prescription pills laced with fentanyl have contributed to thousands of fatal overdoses across the country. The unpredictability of these substances has made drug use more dangerous than ever before.

New synthetic drugs continue to emerge, further exacerbating the crisis. Carfentanil, a synthetic opioid 10,000 times stronger than morphine, has been linked to numerous overdose deaths. Another dangerous substance, U-47700 (nicknamed "pink"), mimics the effects of heroin and has caused dozens of fatalities. These synthetic drugs are often sold online or disguised as other substances, making them difficult to regulate and control.

The overdose epidemic has reached catastrophic levels in the United States. Overdose is now the leading cause of injury-related death in the country. From 2000 to 2015, drug overdose deaths more than doubled, and deaths involving opioids more than tripled. By 2017, synthetic opioids were responsible for the majority of overdose fatalities, underscoring the deadly impact of fentanyl and similar substances.

The rate of drug poisoning deaths has risen dramatically over the past two decades. In 2000, the death rate from drug overdoses was 6.2 per 100,000 people. By 2015, that number had jumped to 16.3 per 100,000. The sheer scale of the crisis has overwhelmed hospitals, rehabilitation centers, and law enforcement agencies, leaving communities struggling to cope with the consequences.

One of the most alarming aspects of the crisis is the role of counterfeit pills. Many users purchase prescription opioids on the black market, unaware that these pills may be fake and laced with fentanyl or other lethal substances. This trend has led to an increase in accidental overdoses, as individuals consume what they believe to be legitimate medication but instead ingest a far more potent and deadly drug.

The rise in overdose deaths has placed significant strain on first responders and healthcare providers. Emergency medical personnel frequently encounter cases where individuals require multiple doses of naloxone, a medication used to reverse opioid overdoses. The potency of fentanyl and other synthetic opioids has made it increasingly difficult to save lives, even with prompt medical intervention.

In addition to the health risks, the opioid crisis has had profound social and economic consequences. Families are being torn apart by addiction, communities are experiencing surges in crime, and the costs of treating opioid dependency and overdoses are placing immense burdens on healthcare systems. The ripple effects of the crisis extend far beyond those who use drugs, affecting entire neighborhoods and cities.

While government agencies continue to fight drug trafficking and implement public health initiatives, the crisis shows no signs of slowing down. The evolving nature of drug smuggling, the increasing presence of synthetic opioids, and the widespread availability of adulterated substances make it clear that more comprehensive solutions are needed. Without aggressive intervention, the number of overdose deaths will likely continue to rise, further devastating communities across the nation.

The opioid epidemic is not just a law enforcement issue—it is a public health emergency that requires a multi-faceted response. Expanding access to addiction treatment, increasing public education on the dangers of synthetic opioids, and strengthening international efforts to curb drug trafficking are all critical steps in addressing this crisis. The future of millions of Americans depends on finding effective solutions to combat one of the deadliest drug epidemics in history.

The future of the War on Drugs is likely to be shaped by ongoing debates over legalization, harm reduction, and racial justice. While significant progress has been made in shifting drug policy away from punitive measures, challenges remain in ensuring that reforms are implemented equitably. The fight for criminal justice reform, public health-focused drug policies, and racial equity will continue to shape the evolving landscape of drug enforcement in the United States.

Chapter 4

Bitch Imma Crackbaby!

It does not matter who my father was to you. Who he was to me matters more.

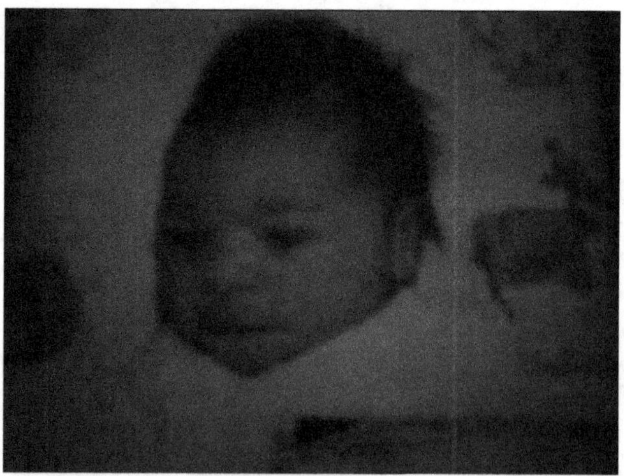

My father was born somewhere on the South Side of Chicago in the summer of 1973. Exactly where he was born, I do not know. What I do know is that he was one of four boys born to my grandmother, a woman who did her best to raise her children despite the challenges she faced. Whether my father ever knew his own father or grandfather remains unclear, but given the circumstances, it is likely that he grew up without a father figure in his life. His childhood, marked by instability and absence, set the foundation for many of the struggles he would later face.

The story of my father's youth is one I am all too familiar with. As one of three boys born to my mother, I, too, experienced the absence of my biological father. His presence in my life was like a shadow—always there, yet never quite visible. His battle with substance abuse ensured that our relationship was one of distance and disappointment. The grip of addiction dragged him through a revolving door of incarceration, leaving little room for fatherhood. Instead of bedtime stories and life lessons, he brought with him tales of prison cells and missed opportunities.

The absence of my father created a void that extended beyond the physical. It was an emotional, psychological, and even spiritual absence that left deep scars. While other children had fathers to teach them how to ride a bike, throw a football, or navigate the complexities of life, I had to figure things out on my own. The streets became my classroom, and my mistakes were my teachers. His love for the streets and drugs had placed an unbridgeable chasm between us, leaving me with unanswered questions and unresolved pain.

Despite his absence, I was fortunate enough to have a stepfather who stepped in and took on the role my biological father had abandoned. My stepfather did not have to take responsibility for me, yet he did so without hesitation. He provided the stability and guidance I desperately needed, and for that, I am forever grateful. He showed me that being a father is about presence, not just biology. Through him, I learned what it meant to be a man, not by blood, but by action and commitment.

My father's struggles extended beyond his personal demons; they were also tied to his lack of education. According to my mother, he dropped out of elementary school, a decision that had lifelong consequences. Without education, his opportunities were limited, his choices were narrow, and his future was largely determined by circumstance rather than ambition. The streets became his teacher, and crime became his curriculum. With no diploma and no skills to fall back on, he was left with few options but to repeat the same cycles of destruction he had known all his life.

His life was a series of poor choices and reckless decisions, leading him down a predictable path of hardship. Given his background, it would not surprise me if he had joined a gang. Many young men in similar situations seek out gangs in search of identity, belonging, and protection. However, the security gangs promise is an illusion; they offer nothing but a faster route to prison, violence, or an early grave. If my father had indeed chosen that path, it would only have deepened the chaos that already consumed his life.

Despite his shortcomings, I do not write this to vilify my father but to understand him. His life is a cautionary tale, a reminder of the dangers of neglect, addiction, and the absence of guidance. He was a man trapped in cycles that began long before he was born. The pain he caused was not just his own but something that rippled through generations, shaping the lives of his children, including me. In many ways, his failures have been my greatest lessons, teaching me what not to do, who not to become, and why breaking the cycle is so important.

Today, I stand as a man determined not to let my past define me. I have taken my father's absence and turned it into a motivation to be present. Where he failed, I strive to succeed. His story does not have to be my story. I choose to walk a different path, one paved with purpose, resilience, and a commitment to change. If nothing else, my father's life has taught me that I have the power to break the cycle and create a legacy of strength, wisdom, and love.

Growing up without my father's presence left a wound that never fully healed. It was not just about the missed birthdays or the empty chairs at school events—it was the deep, lingering question of why. Why wasn't I enough for him to stay? Why didn't he fight harder to be in my life? And as I grew into a man, I vowed that my children would never have to ask themselves those same painful questions. They would never have to search for me in the faces of strangers or wonder what it felt like to be held by their father. Yet, as much as I try to be everything he was not, I find myself wrestling with the harsh reality that in some ways, I am him.

I work tirelessly—grinding, hustling, sacrificing—because I refuse to let my children experience the struggles I did. My father left me with nothing but questions, so I break my back making sure my kids have everything. But the irony in my effort is painful: in trying to secure their future, I am slowly fading from their present. I am so caught up in providing that I forget that sometimes, what they need most is just for me to be there. Not as a provider, not as a protector, but simply as Dad—sitting next to them on the couch, watching a movie, laughing, or helping with a school project.

There is a deeper, darker side to this. Absence is absence, no matter the reason behind it. My father was gone because he chose to be, and I am gone because I choose to work—but at the end of the day, my children only feel the distance. The result is the same: a father who is not there. The guilt eats at me because I know better. I know what it feels like to grow up without a father, to feel like a piece of you is missing, and yet, I am inadvertently creating that same void in my children's lives. It's a bitter pill to swallow when you realize that, despite your best efforts, history has a way of repeating itself.

Looking in the mirror is a battle. Some days, I see a man who is breaking generational curses, a father who works tirelessly to build a better life for his kids. Other days, I see the reflection of the man I swore I had never become—a father who is not home enough, isn't present enough, isn't enough. And the hardest part? My kids don't care about the long hours, the paychecks, or the sacrifices—I see it in their eyes. They just want me. Not the provider, not the hustler, just Dad.

I know deep down that love is not just about what you give but how you show up. No amount of money, gifts, or a nice house can replace the feeling of presence. I do not want my children to remember me as the dad who worked hard but was never really there. I do not want them to look back on their childhood and feel the same emptiness that I do when I think of mine. I want to be both—the provider and the present father. But damn, that balance is hard.

So, where do I go from here? The first step is acknowledgment, and I see my flaws clearer than ever. I know that no matter how much I work, time is the one thing I can never get back. My children will not always be this young. One day, they will stop asking me to play with them, stop running to me with their excitement, and I'll regret every single moment I let slip away. I can't afford to let that happen. The grind is important, but my presence is priceless.

I have to make a change—not just for them, but for me. Because if I continue down this path, I will be the very thing I resent most. And that is a burden my heart cannot bear. My father's absence is a trauma I will always carry, but it doesn't have to be the legacy I leave behind. My children deserve better. I deserve better. It's time to break the cycle—before it's too late.

And so, I say this to myself as much as to them: I see you. I love you. And I am going to do better. Because no amount of hard work will ever be more valuable than simply being here.

"And he will turn The hearts of the fathers to the children, And the hearts of the children to their fathers, Lest I come and strike the earth with a curse".
—Holy Bible (Malachi 4:6)

Attachment theory explains how our earliest relationships shape the way we connect with others throughout life. Developed by psychologist John Bowlby and expanded by Mary Ainsworth, this theory suggests that the bonds we form in childhood—especially with our caregivers—set the foundation for our emotional security and ability to form relationships. When these bonds are strong, a child learns that the world is safe, love is reliable, and relationships can be trusted. But when those bonds are broken, inconsistent, or outright absent, the child adapts in ways that can lead to deep emotional struggles in adulthood. Avoidant attachment, one of the primary insecure attachment styles, often develops in response to emotional neglect or abandonment.

I know that avoidant attachment is something I struggle with because my father was absent due to his addiction to drugs and alcohol. His addiction took priority over being a father, leaving me to navigate the world without the security of his love and guidance. As a child, I internalized this abandonment, not just as a failure on his part, but as something wrong with me. When a parent is absent, especially due to addiction, a child does not understand that it is the addiction that causes the absence—they only feel the void. To protect myself from the pain of that loss, I learned to shut off my emotions, to rely only on myself, and to believe that needing love or connection was dangerous.

Avoidant attachment is characterized by a fear of emotional closeness and a tendency to avoid deep, vulnerable connections. People like me, who develop this attachment style, often pride themselves on their independence, convincing themselves that they do not need anyone. But beneath that surface, there is a lingering fear of rejection, abandonment, and betrayal. It is not that I don't want love or connection—it's that I struggle to believe it will last. After all, the first man who was supposed to love me chose substances over me. That message became the foundation of how I view relationships: people leave, love is unreliable, and it's safer to keep walls up than to let anyone in.

This manifests in my personal life in ways that are both subtle and deeply damaging. I often struggle with vulnerability, finding it difficult to express my emotions even to those I care about most. I keep people at arm's length, not because I do not love them, but because a part of me fears that if I let them too close, they will leave—just like my father did. I struggle with fully trusting that others will stay, so I often adopt a mindset of self-sufficiency to an extreme degree. I tell myself I do not need help, I don't need support, I don't need love. But deep down, I do. I always have.

One of the hardest things about avoidant attachment is that it does not just affect romantic relationships—it impacts parenting, friendships, and even my relationship with myself. As a father, I see how this attachment style plays out in my life. Because I grew up with an absent father, I work myself to the bone to make sure my kids never experience the kind of struggle I did. But in doing so, I sometimes repeat the same emotional absence that hurt me. I provide for my children materially, but emotionally, I know there are times when I am distant—too busy, too preoccupied, too exhausted to be fully present. It's a cycle that is painful to acknowledge, but necessary to break.

Avoidant attachment also makes it difficult to ask for help. Growing up without my father, I learned to rely only on myself, so admitting that I need support feels foreign and uncomfortable. I struggle to reach out, even when I am drowning. I push through pain and stress alone because, in my mind, needing help feels like a weakness—a dangerous vulnerability that could lead to disappointment. This makes healing even harder, because healing requires connection, openness, and trust—all things that feel unnatural to someone with an avoidant attachment style.

I also see how this attachment style affects my emotions. Avoidant individuals often suppress their feelings, not allowing themselves to fully experience pain, sadness, or even deep love. When emotions become overwhelming, my instinct is to shut down, to withdraw, to distract myself with work, responsibilities, or even just isolation. This is a coping mechanism I learned as a child—when love felt uncertain, I learned to protect myself by pretending I did not need it. But in adulthood, this emotional distance can be damaging, making it hard to truly connect with those who matter most.

Despite these struggles, I know that healing is possible. Avoidant attachment is not a life sentence—it is a defense mechanism that can be unlearned with time, effort, and self-awareness. The first step is acknowledging the wounds that led to this attachment style. I have to remind myself that my father's addiction and absence were not a reflection of my worth. His choices were his own, and they do not define me. Understanding this helps me separate my past from my present, allowing me to make different choices for my own children.

The next step is learning to embrace vulnerability. This means allowing myself to be open with my emotions, even when it feels uncomfortable. It means expressing love freely, not just through providing, but through presence, affection, and emotional connection. It means being there for my children, not just as a provider, but as a father who listens, who plays, who nurtures. The more I allow myself to be emotionally available, the more I break the cycle of abandonment that I inherited.

Another part of healing is seeking support. Whether through therapy, close friendships, or even self-reflection, I have to remind myself that I do not have to do everything alone. Connection is not a weakness—it is a fundamental human need. My father's absence may have taught me to be independent, but I can teach myself something new: that love is safe, that people can be trusted, and that I am worthy of deep, meaningful relationships.

Most importantly, I have to show up differently for my children. I do not want them to grow up questioning my love the way I questioned my father's. I do not want them to feel like they have to earn my presence. I want them to know, without a doubt, that I am here—not just in the financial sense, but in the emotional sense too. My past does not have to dictate my future, and while avoidant attachment may be a struggle, it is not an identity. I am more than my trauma. I am a father, a protector, a provider—but most of all, I am someone who is willing to heal.

Healing avoidant attachment is not easy, but I owe it to myself, and more importantly, to my children. They deserve a father who is present in every way. And I deserve to experience the love I was denied as a child. The cycle ends with me.

In 1991my father criminal enterprise started. He received a class four felony on one count which landed him a two-year prison sentence for possession of an unauthorized controlled substance. A controlled substance is a drug or chemical that a government regulates for its manufacture, possession, and use. This includes prescription medications that are chosen by law, as well as illicitly used drugs.

Two years later my father was back at it again, this time his charges were much more serious. Unlike the last charge, this time he was convicted for one count of a class one felony for possession of controlled substance with the intent to sell or deliver. Due to this he would spend the next four years of his life in prison. Even though he was caught and convicted his actions could have ruined someone else's life.

Now according to his sentencing information sheet, it shows him committing another crime three years later which leads me to believe he might have been released early. Unlike his last two convictions my father found himself being convicted for six more years for being in possession of a stolen vehicle.

My mother did a wonderful job protecting me from his unsafe lifestyle. She would always say "if you ever visit your grandmother do not get in a car if your father is driving unless you guys are with your grandmother." My mother knew something that at the time I did not understand. Speaking of my mother, I never heard her speak of the jailbird negatively, knowing the jailbird personally and his criminal background she never stopped me from having a relationship with him.

My father became a thief to support his substance abuse habit. After being released, in 1999 he was convicted and sentence to one year in prison for retail theft. Knowing how substance users operate I am quite sure his thought process was to steal, sell and get high.

In 2001 he was back convicted and sentence to two years of possession of controlled substance.

Not even a year later my father found him back incarcerated serving a six-year prison sentence for burglary. This was his second class two felony and obviously not his last time going to prison. Somehow, this last prison experience must have taught him a lesson because he had managed to stay out of prison for the next twelve in which I have no memory of spending any time with him.

I would often reach out to check in with him, but he would never really talk about shit. Hoping that he would explain to me the reason behind his actions and his absence. In fact, I got the total opposite. I felt like a burden continuously reaching out and not getting anywhere with him.

In 2014 I was out of college and officially a man. I had my first child, and he was a grandparent. Unfortunately, I never met any of my grandfathers if I had to guess I would say my father probably did not have a relationship with his father. I remember but sure exactly how we contacted one another, and he came to visit out the blue. From an earlier visit year ago, my father was almost unrecognizable to me. I could tell it was the drugs he had been using; we spent about an hour together I was confused and did not understand why now. Shortly after the visit my father was back incarcerated serving a one-year prison sentence for possession of controlled substance.

Honestly, I was mad at myself that I did not try harder to save this man from himself. When I finally saw him, I looked him in face and said, "dude you should be tired of this shit and living like this." I did not know severity of the crime he had committed. I later found out that he was getting ready to serve an eighteen-year prison sentence for criminal sexual assault.

During the 1980s and 1990s, the opioid epidemic and the broader War on Drugs led to a significant rise in drug-related arrests, jail and prison populations, and the number of men in halfway houses in Chicago. The impact was particularly severe for African American communities, as drug laws disproportionately targeted Black men.

By the mid-1990s, nearly one in three African American men aged 20 to 29 in the U.S. was under some form of correctional supervision, including probation, parole, or incarceration. In 1996, one in every 20 Black men was in state or federal prison, compared to one in every 180 white men. The racial disparity in incarceration was stark, with Black men being imprisoned at rates 13 times higher than their white counterparts.

In Chicago, aggressive drug policing led to a massive increase in arrests, particularly for possession offenses. African Americans were disproportionately affected, making up 78% of those arrested, 89% of those convicted, and 92% of those jailed for low-level drug possession, despite evidence that drug use rates were similar across racial groups. The disparity was especially pronounced in neighborhoods with high concentrations of Black residents, where arrest rates were up to 150 times higher than in predominantly white areas.

Chicago's Cook County Jail became one of the largest single-site jails in the country, with a population exceeding 10,000 inmates at times. A significant portion of this population consisted of individuals arrested for nonviolent drug offenses. The introduction of mandatory minimum sentences and harsh penalties for crack cocaine possession—used more frequently in Black communities—exacerbated the problem. In 1992, African Americans comprised 12% of the U.S. population but accounted for 75% of those sentenced to prison for drug possession.

State prisons in Illinois reflected this trend. By 2001, African Americans made up 46% of Illinois' prison population, even though they comprised a much smaller percentage of the general population. The racial disparities extended to probation, with 31% of African Americans under supervision compared to 55% of white individuals. The sentencing disparity between powder and crack cocaine played a significant role in these numbers, with nearly 90% of those sentenced for crack-related offenses being Black.

Halfway houses in Chicago also saw an increase in residents, as many men were released from prison under parole supervision. These facilities, often meant for reintegration and addiction treatment, housed a disproportionate number of Black men affected by mandatory sentencing laws. Drug courts and alternative sentencing programs emerged in the late 1990s to address the crisis, but these efforts were often underfunded and had limited reach.

The effects of mass incarceration from this era continue to impact Chicago's Black communities today. Many families were left fatherless, economic opportunities were stifled, and the cycle of incarceration persisted across generations. The War on Drugs' legacy remains a critical issue in discussions of criminal justice reform and racial equity in Chicago and beyond.

The opioid epidemic has had devastating consequences for families across the United States, leaving countless children without the presence and support of their fathers. As addiction takes hold, many fathers find themselves unable to fulfill their parental responsibilities, leading to emotional and physical abandonment. The crisis has not only torn families apart but has also created long-term social and psychological consequences for the children left behind. Understanding the impact of opioid addiction on fatherhood requires examining the economic, legal, and emotional factors that drive fathers away from their children.

Opioid addiction fundamentally alters a person's brain chemistry, making the pursuit of the drug the most pressing priority in their lives. Fathers who become addicted often begin neglecting their responsibilities, as their cravings and withdrawal symptoms overshadow everything else. What starts as a prescription for pain relief can quickly turn into dependency, and soon, obtaining the next dose takes precedence over being present for their children. As addiction deepens, fathers may disappear for extended periods, leaving their children confused, hurt, and longing for their presence.

Many fathers struggling with opioid addiction experience severe financial hardship, which exacerbates family instability. Addiction often leads to job loss due to absenteeism, poor performance, or workplace accidents. Without a steady income, many fathers can no longer provide for their children, leading to eviction, homelessness, and, in some cases, incarceration. With nowhere to turn, some fathers simply disappear, believing that their children are better off without them. This financial instability leaves many single mothers, grandparents, or other relatives to pick up the pieces, struggling to provide for the children left behind.

The criminalization of drug addiction has played a significant role in separating fathers from their children. Many fathers who struggle with opioid use are arrested for possession, distribution, or crimes committed to sustain their addiction, such as theft. The U.S. has some of the harshest drug laws in the world, leading to lengthy prison sentences even for nonviolent offenses. Once incarcerated, fathers lose contact with their children, sometimes for years. Even after release, reuniting with their children can be difficult due to legal barriers, social stigma, and the deep wounds left by their absence.

When a father becomes addicted to opioids, child protective services (CPS) often step in to remove children from unstable or unsafe homes. This intervention, while necessary in cases of neglect or abuse, can lead to permanent family separations. Fathers who lose custody due to addiction may struggle to regain parental rights, especially if they lack the resources for legal representation or rehabilitation. Many children end up in foster care or being raised by relatives, further diminishing the chances of reunification with their fathers.

Children of opioid-addicted fathers often suffer from deep emotional wounds due to feelings of abandonment and rejection. Many struggle with questions like, "Why wasn't I enough for my father to stay?" This sense of loss can lead to issues such as depression, anxiety, low self-esteem, and difficulty forming healthy relationships. Some children blame themselves for their father's absence, leading to feelings of guilt and shame that persist into adulthood.

Studies show that children of addicted parents are at a significantly higher risk of developing substance use disorders themselves. Without a stable father figure, many children turn to drugs and alcohol as a coping mechanism for the trauma they endured. This creates a vicious cycle, where addiction and family breakdown repeat across generations. Without intervention, many of these children will follow the same destructive path as their fathers, perpetuating the epidemic.

With fathers absent due to opioid addiction, the burden of parenting often falls on single mothers and grandparents. Single mothers must navigate the emotional and financial challenges of raising children alone, while many grandparents step in to provide stability. However, this added responsibility can be overwhelming, especially for elderly grandparents who may struggle with health and financial limitations. The strain on extended family members can lead to burnout, stress-related illnesses, and even family breakdowns.

Many addicted fathers feel an overwhelming sense of shame and guilt for the pain they have caused their children. This guilt often leads them to avoid contact, believing their children would be better off without them. Rather than seeking help, they may isolate themselves further, deepening the divide between them and their children. Unfortunately, this self-imposed exile does little to alleviate the pain felt by both the father and child.

One of the most tragic outcomes of the opioid epidemic is the high number of overdose deaths among fathers. Many addicted fathers never get the chance to rebuild their lives because their addiction ultimately takes their lives. Children who lose their fathers to overdoses often struggle with unresolved grief, leading to long-term mental health issues. The trauma of losing a parent in such a way can shape a child's entire life, making it difficult for them to trust or form stable relationships.

Even when fathers seek help, the road to recovery is difficult. Many addiction treatment programs are expensive or have long waiting lists, making access to care difficult. Those who do complete rehabilitation often face barriers when trying to reconnect with their children, such as legal restrictions, financial instability, or mistrust from the child's mother or guardians. Without strong support systems, many fathers relapse, leading to a cycle of temporary reunification followed by renewed abandonment.

Some organizations have stepped in to help addicted fathers reclaim their roles in their children's lives. Faith-based recovery programs, mentorship initiatives, and community support groups offer guidance, treatment, and reintegration assistance. Programs that focus on both addiction recovery and fatherhood education can be instrumental in breaking the cycle of abandonment. However, these programs often lack sufficient funding and resources to reach all the fathers who need them.

Addressing the opioid epidemic's impact on fatherhood requires systemic policy changes. Instead of treating addiction primarily as a criminal issue, there needs to be a greater focus on rehabilitation, mental health treatment, and economic opportunities. Expanding access to affordable treatment centers, job training programs, and family reunification initiatives could help more fathers reclaim their roles in their children's lives.

The widespread abandonment of children by opioid-addicted fathers has long-term consequences for society. Fatherless children are statistically more likely to experience poverty, drop out of school, engage in criminal behavior, and struggle with addiction themselves. The opioid epidemic is not just a personal or family crisis—it is a societal crisis that affects entire communities.

While the opioid epidemic has left many children without fathers, there is still hope for change. Through increased awareness, support for recovery programs, and compassionate policy changes, more fathers can be given the chance to heal and rebuild relationships with their children. Providing second chances, rather than lifelong punishment, can help break the cycle of addiction and abandonment.

CHAPTER 5

Unmasking the Deceiver

"LOOK OUT MARLON, SAY CHEESE"
"LOOKING ASS BOY"

Here is the actual mugshot of my stupid ass detained in Starke County Department of Corrections. This photo was taken directly from their website back in 2016.

"The blindfold on Justice's eyes is not a symbol of impartiality, but a representation of a system that will fully ignores the inequities it perpetuates. For in the name of justice, we often turn a blind eye to the injustices that stare us straight in the face."

Orange is considered to be a spirited color that exists between red and yellow on the color spectrum. It holds a remarkable place in human history, spirituality, psychology, and nature. Often associated with warmth, energy, creativity, and the sun, orange is a color that commands attention and radiates positivity. Right now, we will delve into its history, spiritual significance, emotional impact, and connection to the sun while also addressing its creation and symbolic importance.

The history of orange as a recognized color dates back thousands of years, originating in nature and cultural developments long before the term "orange" was coined. Early humans met orange in the form of natural materials like ochre, a type of earth pigment used in prehistoric cave paintings. Some of the oldest examples of ochre pigment use date back to at least 75,000 years ago, as discovered in Blombos Cave, South Africa. This earthy tone became one of the first pigments humans used for art and decoration.

The color we now know as orange did not have a specific name in many early languages. For centuries, it was simply referred to as a shade of red or yellow. The term "orange" as a color appeared in Europe during the Middle Ages. It was derived from the Old French word orenge, which came from the Arabic nāranj, referring to the fruit brought to Europe by traders from Asia. By the 16th century, the word "orange" was being used to describe both the fruit and the color in English.

The creation of orange pigments for artistic purposes

began in ancient times. Natural materials such as realgar (a mineral rich in arsenic sulfide) and orpiment were used by ancient Egyptians and other civilizations to produce bright orange hues. These substances were prized for their vibrant color but were toxic, requiring careful handling.

In the medieval period, orange pigments were also created from plant-based sources, such as saffron or marigold petals, though these tended to fade over time. With the development of synthetic pigments in the 19th century, artists gained access to more stable and vivid orange tones, significantly expanding the color's use in art and design.

Orange carries deep spiritual significance across various cultures and traditions. Its warm, glowing essence symbolizes balance, creativity, and transformation, making it a dominant color in many spiritual practices.

In Hinduism and Buddhism, orange holds a sacred place. Saffron robes worn by Buddhist monks and Hindu priests symbolize renunciation, purity, and spiritual enlightenment. The choice of orange reflects a detachment from materialism and a focus on spiritual growth. In these traditions, the color is associated with the rising sun, standing for a new beginning and the cycle of life.

In chakra theory, orange is associated with the sacral chakra (Svadhisthana), found in the lower abdomen. This energy center governs creativity, passion, and emotions, making orange a symbol of vitality and self-expression. A balanced sacral chakra is believed to foster a sense of joy, sensuality, and connection to others.

Orange also plays a role in spiritual practices beyond Eastern traditions. In Celtic spirituality, orange was linked to the harvest season, symbolizing abundance, and the warmth of the sun. In modern metaphysical practices, orange is used in meditation to stimulate creativity and remove emotional blockages.

The psychological effects of orange are complex, as the color can evoke a range of emotions depending on its shade and context. As a warm color, orange tends to stimulate and energize, creating feelings of enthusiasm and excitement.

While orange is associated with positive emotions, it can also be overwhelming in certain contexts. Bright orange tones can sometimes feel too intense or aggressive, leading to feelings of restlessness or irritation if overused.

Diverse cultures perceive orange in unique ways. In Western cultures, it is often linked to autumn, Halloween, and harvest festivals, carrying connotations of change and transition. In contrast, in Asian cultures, orange may represent happiness and prosperity.

As a natural color, orange has existed since the dawn of time, visible in the fiery glow of the sun, the vibrant petals of flowers, and the rinds of citrus fruits. However, the deliberate creation of orange as a pigment or dye can be traced back to ancient civilizations.

The Egyptians were among the first to create orange pigments using orpiment, a mineral that yielded a brilliant golden-orange hue. They used it for decorative purposes in art, jewelry, and burial tombs. Similarly, the Romans and Greeks used natural ochre and plant-based dyes to achieve orange tones in their artworks.

The development of synthetic orange pigments began in the 19th century during the Industrial Revolution. Chemists discovered new methods to produce stable, non-toxic pigments, such as cadmium orange, which became a favorite among artists like Vincent van Gogh.

Orange is more than just a visually striking color—it carries profound importance in various aspects of life, from cultural symbolism to practical applications.

Orange has been a significant color in art, used by painters to convey warmth and emotion. For example, van Gogh's use of orange and complementary blues in his works created a sense of vibrancy and harmony. In modern design, orange is a popular choice for its ability to draw attention and create a sense of fun and creativity.

Orange fruits and vegetables, such as carrots, oranges, and pumpkins, are rich in beta-carotene and vitamin C, essential nutrients for human health. The color orange in food often signals vitality and nourishment.

Orange shares an intrinsic connection with the sun, embodying its warmth, energy, and life-giving properties. The sun itself often appears orange at sunrise and sunset due to the scattering of light in the atmosphere, making orange a natural symbol of the sun's beauty and power.

In many cultures, the sun is a symbol of life, growth, and renewal. Orange captures these qualities, representing the radiant energy that sustains life on Earth. This connection is especially clear in agricultural societies, where the orange hues of ripened crops and autumn leaves mirror the sun's nurturing role.

Just as the sun fuels life, orange is a source of creative and emotional energy. Its association with the sun makes it a color of inspiration, capable of sparking innovative ideas and encouraging bold action.

Orange is a multifaceted hue that transcends mere aesthetics, weaving its way into the fabric of history, spirituality, psychology, and nature. From its ancient origins in earth pigments to its sacred role in Eastern traditions, orange has consistently represented creativity, warmth, and transformation. Emotionally, it energizes and uplifts, while its connection to the sun highlights its role as a symbol of life and vitality.

Through the ages, orange has continued to inspire and captivate, proving that it is far more than just a color—it is a powerful force that shapes the way we experience the world. Whether in the glow of a sunset, the zest of a citrus fruit, or the robes of a monk, orange reminds us of the beauty and dynamism of life.

Ode to Orange

Orange is the fire that sets dawn aglow,
A blaze in the sky where the warm breezes blow.
It is the crackle of leaves in the crisp autumn air,
The spice in the cider, the pumpkins with care.

It is the sun sinking low in a fiery embrace,
A burst of pure energy, a fearless new face.
It is laughter and courage, a wild, restless spark,
A lantern of hope in the velvety dark.

It dances in fields where the marigolds sway,
A whisper of warmth on a cold winter's day.
It hums in the rust of a weathered old door,
The glow of adventure that calls us for more.

It is the flicker of flames in a passionate heart,
The ember of dreams that refuse to depart.
Orange is daring, both fierce and divine,
A color of power, of spirit, of time.

Fuck The Color Orange!

The Curse of Orange

Oh, wretched hue that burns my sight,
A blinding blaze, too loud, too bright.
Like caution tape and warning signs,
A garish glow that twists and binds.

It stains the sky at setting sun,
A fire that mocks when day is done.
Its clash with calm, its war with peace,
A color that will never cease.

The pumpkin's grin, a hollow sneer,
Its autumn reign, I do not cheer.
The citrus bite, the harsh embrace,
A shade that never shows me grace.

Oh, orange, loud and crude and vile,
Your brazen tone, your garish style.
If colors spoke, you would always scream—
A neon nightmare, not a dream.

Orange is often associated with vibrancy and warmth, which evokes a vastly different emotional response in people. The instant I lay eyes on the color, I am transported back to a bleak and hopeless place a fucking jail cell, where I was falsely incarcerated. That prisoner's uniform I was forced to wear, was a faded orange jumpsuit that fitted me perfectly. That shit is forever stuck in my memory as a symbol of oppression, shame, and loss of freedom.

However, I wore that uniform proudly. The harsh fluorescent lights cast unforgiving shadows as I strided down the concrete corridor, my footsteps echoing in the sterile silence.

The cold, institutional grey walls close in, the only color the faded, chipped paint and the occasional glimpse of a barred cell door. My posture was a stark contrast to the casual swagger of a model on a runway. My head was held high, not with confidence, but with a forced defiance.

Every step was calculated, a silent declaration of survival in my face of overwhelming odds. The catwalk stretched out before me, a path leading to an uncertain future, a cell block was my final destination.

But orange holds an even deeper significance for me. It was the last color I saw from the free world before the sally port door closed behind me, marking the beginning of my journey into the unknown. As I stood in the bright sunlight, waiting to be processed into the prison system, I looked up at the sky and was struck by the intense orange hue of the sun. It was as if the color was seared into my retina, a lasting reminder of the freedom I was about to lose.

In that moment, I remember thinking to myself that this process was going to be long and arduous. Orange symbolized the uncertainty and fear that gripped my heart. It was as if the color was a harbinger of the challenges that lay ahead, a reminder that my life was about to take a drastic turn.

That uniform, with its dull, washed-out color, felt like a physical manifestation of my lost autonomy. Every time I put it on, I felt like I was being shackled, not just physically, but also emotionally. The course, rough fabric seemed to chafe against my skin, a constant reminder of my confinement. The uniform smelled old and musty, like it had been worn by countless others before me, each with their own stories of struggle and hardship.

When I think of orange, I am reminded of the dehumanizing experience of wearing that uniform. It was as if I had been reduced to a mere number, a statistic in a system that seemed designed to break my spirit. Orange represents the loss of my identity, my freedom, and my dignity.

But orange is not just a visual reminder of my incarceration; it also evokes a powerful sense of smell. The prisoner's uniform reeked of stale sweat, dirty laundry, and the acrid smell of disinfectant. It was as if the uniform had absorbed the collective stench of the prison, a noxious odor that clung to me like a bad omen. Every time I caught a whiff of that smell, I felt like I was being transported back to that cold, unforgiving place.

One of the most vivid memories I have of my time in prison is the taste of that uniform. In a moment of desperation and rage, I bit down on the sleeve of my shirt, the rough fabric tearing against my teeth. The taste was bitter and metallic, like blood and tears mixed. It was as if I could taste the collective suffering of all those who had worn that uniform before me.

Orange will forever be linked in my mind with the trauma of false incarceration. It represents the loss of my freedom, my dignity, and my sense of self. Every time I see orange; I am reminded of the pain and the suffering that I endured during that dark period in my life. Orange may be vibrant and warm to some, but to me, it will always be a painful reminder of a traumatic experience that has left an indelible mark on my life.

Back when I was a young whippersnapper, my friends and I would often taunt, prank, and make fun of the neighborhood junkies. We saw them as outsiders, weak and flawed. But little did we understand the grip of their addiction. Junkies use to be the target pray for our foolish and immature mentality, on days like Halloween they would become a victim to a full carton of relentless egg throwing. Shit, depending on the day and the crew I have seen some of my friends just walk up and punch they ass directly in the face. Sending them straight to the ground unconscious, lifeless. I know that was harsh but to us as kids that shit was the high light of the day.

One thing for sure, we depended on the junkies to come trough for us. For example, if we needed anything that we could not get personally guess who we counted on, yep, the same junkies we targeted. Truthfully, I do not even know why we found them that interesting enough in the first place. Now that I am older, I remember looking into their eyes and nothing was there, but they were some of the friendliest and nicest people I ever met. Although we did not trust them, we bene-fited tremendously from them.

I wonder if anyone ever viewed my father that way. Nonetheless, substance abuse and alcohol addiction are destructive forces that ravage lives, reputations, and families. They creep in silently, masquerading as temporary escapes, only to ensnare victims in cycles of dependence.

For those junkies, addiction stole their dignity, leaving them individuals vulnerable to exploitation and manipulation. It destroyed their relationships, eroding trust, and love. Most of the junkies I met, suffered from the consequences of their life-style with health problems, organ damage, infections, and cognitive impairment, financial ruin, depleted savings, lost jobs, debt, legal troubles, arrests, incarceration, and severed ties, social isolation, estrangement from loved ones and the commu-nity. It is sickening to know my friends and I found laughter and joy from adding an ass whooping to their pain.

Have we forgotten that addiction is a disease, not a choice. We overlook the complexities of mental health, trauma, and environment that contribute to substance abuse. Did we ever stop to think what was they life like before the drugs and alco-hol? Did we ever care enough to ask them were they ok? Society often views those struggling with addiction as failures, morally flawed, and weak-willed. This stigma perpetuates shame, silence, and suffering.

Despite taking part in bullying, I felt a pang of compassion for the junkies. I saw the desperation in their eyes, the plea for help. I wanted to understand their struggles.

As I grew older, my empathy deepened. I realized that addiction was not just a personal issue but a societal problem. We need to address root causes, provide support and resources.

I recognize the harm caused by bullying and disrespect. I understand now that addiction demands compassion, not ridicule. After losing my grandmother I had to educate myself on addiction and mental health. I had to start offering support to rehabilitation and treatment initiatives. I am now an Advocate for policy changes addressing addiction. I embrace my empathy and understanding and to those junkies I slap upside they head just for fun or made them steal out the corner store for me I am sorry. That experience has transformed me. I now dedicate myself to helping others overcome addiction I am now their superhero. I stand with them; I thank my grand-mother because her death caused me to be that beacon of light.

I grew up in the harsh, unforgiving reality of South Side Chicago, where poverty, violence and desperation enveloped everyday life. Our neighborhood was a battleground, with families fighting to survive amidst rampant crime and decay. Despite their best efforts, my loved ones struggled to make ends meet, facing impossible choices between paying bills or putting food on the table.

The local schools were underfunded and underperforming, leaving students without access to quality education. Classrooms were overcrowded, resources scarce and expecta-tions low. Textbooks were outdated, and technology nonexistent. It seemed like the system had given up on us, as if our potential were not worth investing in.

Street corners were bustling with people trying to hustle and make a living. Some turned to legitimate means, like selling homemade goods or offering services, while others succumbed to the allure of quick money through drug dealing or other illicit activities. Violence and gang activity cast a constant shadow, with shootings, stabbings and robberies becoming grim routine.

As kids, we looked up to the flashy drug dealers as role models. They had it all: girls, money, cars and clothes. Their lifestyle appeared glamorous, and we wanted in. We would watch them cruise through the neighborhood, music blasting, and think, "That's the life." But amidst the chaos, something within me whispered that this path led nowhere good.

Fortunately, I made better decisions. I chose to focus on education, personal growth, and positivity. I devoured books, joined after-school programs, and found solace in sports. This choice was not always easy; peers mocked me for being "different" and "wanting better" for myself. But it paid off, many of my peers who followed the destructive path now regret their decisions, trapped in cycles of violence, addiction, or incarceration. I bet now they only wish they had made the same decision I made. I always had a dream to be the superstar ball player that would come back to the school and give away toys, money and all that other bullshit that means nothing.

Remarkably, I navigated this treacherous environment with minimal police encounters and peer pressure. I never grew up afraid of anyone, so peer pressure was never going to work. My determination to succeed and innate sense of self-worth shielded me from the toxic influences surrounding me. I knew I deserved better. Sometimes this shit just seems so surreal, let me mother tell it I was a "bad" child, well only bad in certain places like school.

Since we on the topic of school I want to share a little story with you. Until this day I have never told anyone about this so here we go. The only time I ever struggled with the thought using substance was in college. I contemplated repeatedly with myself, I never used but I came extremely close to doing so. Being from the inner city of Chicago south side to be exact I never spent any time around other races. The college I attended was a PWI (predominantly white institution) and since I hated the school with a fucking passion I will not speak of its name. Anyway, majority of the students there were from that community they came from phenomenally successful households. They had no care in the world and would complain about the stupidest shit, there were only a hand full of African American students on campus most of they asses acted the exact same way. I stayed to myself and did not care to make friends or socialize I felt extremely overwhelmed at times, but my competitive nature keeps me going.

This was my first time being on my own and I loved it. The campus was beautiful and peaceful at night I heard no shootings or police sirens and during the day it was birds chirping. I was relieved my entire life was ahead of my and I was was the road to living out my dreams. Every weekend there would a party or two going on somewhere I never attended that shit because I do not fucking drink beer, and I am not a fan of rocking roll. I would see the students walk through campus late nights drunk and high and I never saw myself that way. I did not trust anyone not to say this was happening, but I would always think about the possibility of someone putting a substance in my drink.

My freshman year of college was meant to be a thrilling new chapter, but fate had other plans. Tragedy struck repeatedly, testing my resilience. Within my very first semester, my family and I endured five devastating losses, including my beloved cousin, who was more like a brother, and my cherished uncle, who had taught me invaluable life lessons. These deaths shook me to my core.

The most crushing blow was my cousin's tragic murder at just a teenager. His senseless killing sparked outrage and sorrow, forever etching his memory in my mind. This horrific event ignited a fire within me, fueling my desire to pursue law enforcement as a career. I wanted justice for him and others victimized by violence. His memory drives my aspiration to protect and serve.

The grief was suffocating, sending me into a deep, dark abyss of depression. Despair wrapped around me like a shroud, making everyday tasks feel insurmountable. In my vulnerability, substance abuse beckoned as a tempting escape from anguish. However, something within me resisted. My innate desire to achieve greatness and make my loved ones proud fueled my determination to overcome.

Through sheer willpower and resilience, I battled my inner demons, refusing to surrender to substance use. Instead, I chan-neled my pain into self-improvement and growth. Years have passed, but the weight of my cousin's loss still lingers, haunting me with what-ifs. His dependence on me as a role model fills me with regret; I wish I could have done more to help him realize his dreams. Now, I strive daily to honor his legacy through my future law enforcement career, ensuring his memory lives on.

My cousin was more than just family; he was a brother, a confidant, and a partner in crime. His infectious laughter and mischievous grin could light up any room, and his love for pranks was unmatched. Countless nights were spent at each other's houses, sharing stories, secrets, and dreams. His mother, a pillar of strength and guidance, became a second mother to me.

Our bond was forged through laughter and disagreements, but ultimately, love prevailed. We fought, made up and grew together. In his eyes, I saw unwavering determination and drive to uplift his community. Despite our youth, he taught valuable lessons that shaped me into a better person. His resilience inspired me to face challenges head-on.

Though his passing tempted me to cope through self-destructive means, it taught me strength and resilience. I learned to confront pain, dig deep, and find inner resolve. His legacy lives on, reminding me to cherish life, seek growth and honor his memory by overcoming adversity.

Growing up in South Side Chicago taught me resilience, resourcefulness, and determination. I saw firsthand the devastating consequences of systemic failure and poor choices. Yet, I appeared with hope and resolve. I learned to appreciate the little things, find joy in adversity, and cherish life's beauty.

Hopefully my journey serves as testament that even amidst chaos, individuals can choose a different path. We must address systemic issues, support education, and provide opportunities for youth to break free from cycles of poverty and violence. Community programs, mentorship and resources can empower young people to make better choices.

Looking back, I realize the South Side's harsh realities forged strength within me. Though scars remain, they remind me of the power of choice and resilience. My experiences shaped my purpose: to inspire hope, drive change and prove that a better future is possible. As for me I have beat the odds and still breaking down walls. By the blessings of Allah, I have been able to live a superstar ball player type of lifestyle now I just need to come back and give back.

I will never forget the day my life turned upside down. The

day I was falsely accused of dealing drugs. The day I saw the injustices of the system up close. I was just a regular guy, a father, working hard with two full time jobs, trying to make an honest living, and suddenly I was facing time in prison for a crime I did not commit. As much as I hated that this happened to me, I am so happy it, I learned so much from this event this was the beginning of my purpose.

It started with a trip from Chicago, Illinois to boring ass Muncie, Indiana. I know what y'all thinking "where the fuck is that" to be completely honest I do not fucking know, nor do I care. For the life of me I do not understand, and will I ever accept the fact that the mother of my children made the decision to move away with our children and go there. During her time in Indiana, it seems that I spent more time fighting court case than spending time with my children.

I remember this day like it was yesterday, the weather was very sunny it was warm out with a slight cool breeze of wind. This was unusual weather for February in Chicago. I decided to wear some traditional color army fatigue cargo pants, a dark green hoodie and black leather boots I had gotten from working as a correctional officer in Indiana. I was extremely excited to see my son and daughter. It has been a while since I last heard my kids laugh, eat a hamburger, or just say my name. The week before I worked my last day as a Correctional Officer for the State of Indiana. When I resigned and turned my uniform in and forget to give them back those same rarity ass boots, I was wearing when I got arrested.

If I am not mistaken, my brother had just brought this black Dodge Caliber with black tinted windows. Knowing my current car situation, he allowed me to use his car to pick the kids up for the weekend. The car did smell like cigarettes smoke and there was visibly a tray inside the car filled with ashes. I never like the smell of cigarettes, nor did I ever consume them. The night before, I made two decisions that played a key role in my arrest.

As I got in the car, I notice I did not charge my phone completely in fact my shit was under thirty percent. This was the first fuck up; I quickly exited the car and ran back upstairs into my parent's house to get my phone charger. As I place the phone in my pants pocket, I remember I had a total of three thousand dollars in cash, I had just got paid from both jobs and was going to treat my children to a fun night out. However, I made the decision to only take one thousand dollars with me by the grace of God this decision saved me from having to depend on anyone paying for me to make bail.

Time is moving quickly, and I wanted to get back to Chicago before the sunset. Once I got back outside to hit the road, my children mother brother pulled up and he was going to drive down there with me. After he placed his bags in the vehicle we started our journey to Indiana. The ride was smooth and there were no signs of anything stopping us from making it there safely.

About an hour and half into the ride I notice the GPS on my cell phone which I was using as a guide to direct us to the right location started glitching. Because I was not familiar with this road I just continued driving and thinking that the GPS would get signal again. Unfortunately, it did not and now I was concerned that I might be going in the wrong direction. Out of nowhere the highway I was traveling on started to turn into a two-lane street surrounded by nothing but farmland.

As I am driving, I see and hear police sirens in the distance, between me and you (my readers) I was not about to pull over for shit. Honestly, everything happens so fast, and I was not aware of my speed until I check the speedometer and notice I was driving my brother shit like a race car. "Fuck it" I said to myself quietly, I am in the middle of nowhere with no witnesses and no excess to the world because of my phone service being compromised. So, I continued driving until I came to a gas station.

I kindly pulled into the gas station and proceeded to exit the vehicle like nothing happened like I was not just driving over the speed limit. The Police officers pulled in right behind me, he exited his vehicle with his hand on his gun, yelling for me to get back into the car. I complied, shaken, thinking it was all a mistake. Now usually when an Officer pulls you over the process is about the same.

They say why they stopped you; they might ask why was you driving the speed, they ask for your driving credentials and then they either let you proceed or issue you a moving violation of some sort. This particular Officer did not do any of that, his first question to me once he arrived at the driver side window was "where is the weed." I laughed and his face and ensured him he lost his mind and had the wring guy. He next asked me from my drivers license which I handed it to him. Looking him in his eyes I felt as if I has jut been pulled over by satin himself. I never met this Officer a day in my life, but his energy and it was not good at all.

Especially after he asked me about weed. He took my drivers license and walked back to hid squad car. It felt like he took hours and hours before he came back and asked me if he could search the vehicle and once everything was cleared, I would be good to go.

With confidence I allowed him to search the vehicle not knowing he had intentions on sabotaging my legacy. He searched the vehicle; he even called the K-9 unit to assist with the search. He found nothing, but still took me away in hand-cuffs, as I was walking away his partner asked me "where did I get the black leather boots from" as if they looked familiar to him. I stated "I worked in Corrections and these boots were part of my uniform. The charges: possession of Marijuana with intent to distribute and Reckless Driving. I knew I was innocent, but no one listened." I felt stupid, I felt like a bitch, I felt like my father. As I drove away in back of the squad car all I kept hearing in my head was my mother voice telling me "You going to be just like yo damn daddy."

"Police interrogation rooms are designed to break you. Bright lights, cold metal tables, and the constant to de threat of violence. They told me, 'You're going down for this, might as well confess.' I refused, but the fear crept in. I had seen the news: unarmed Black men killed by police; their lives discarded like trash. I didn't want to be next."

My willingness to cooperate peacefully with The Knox City Police Department was in my opinion a safe decision to make, not for me put for the police officers. I had developed a sense of range that was becoming uncontrollable, my right hand to God had I been by myself I most definitely would have risked everything just to deliver a mush needed ass whooping to that racist bitch. I was never scared during this encounter, but I was aware of the capabilities of the media and the police departments.

To put things into better perspective for you, in 2015 across America law enforcement officers were responsible for the deaths of forty unarmed African Americans. Now add that with the twenty-two unarmed African Americans murdered by the hands law enforcement officers the following year. I should have been number sixty-three and trust me I would wore that number to my grave like a badge of honor. For months after my arrest I use to nightmares that played over and over in my dreams. I suffered from sleep deprivation due to this event, I never thought about seeking professional help because I did not want to appear weak again. That entire situation was pointless and did not have to end the way it did, but I was lucky, blessed.

Unlike the one African American male from Texas who was

shot and killed by police who "mistake" a cell phone in his hand for a gun. Or the African American teenager from Texas who was shot and killed by police for simply just walking towards the officer. Within that same month another African American from Texas was shot and killed by police because the officer "thought" there was a gun. The fourth victim was another African American male from Washington state was shot and killed by police while just simply sitting in his car no gun was never found. The fifth victim was another African American male from Wisconsin who was shot and killed by police. Lastly, another African American male from Alabama was shot and killed by police for running away from a stop-and-frisk search.

May God have mercy on the souls of these innocent individuals and their families. I choose to show respect, love, and support to those six individuals because they to was harassed and possibly discriminated against by law enforcement officers.

I did not spend much time in the Starke County Jail in fact it was only a couple of hours, and I was out back free but mentally devastated, physically exhausted, emotionally drained but spiritually stable. I wanted revenge, retribution for sure but I know I could not just raise hell physically, so I had to think smart I hired an attorney. The first attorney I hired was African American woman she possessed everything I wanted my attorney to be. She was tough, fearless and on my side. Well at least that is what I thought, I explained to her my case she suggested I turn against my co-defendant and put the blame on him. By doing this she explained that I would walk away free from everything. That bitch lost her mind, my co-defendant is family, I love that guy like a brother I was never going to do that. So, I fired her ass, so told me that I was making a mistake not doing what she advised, and I should reconsider. I wanted this to go away but my pride, honor and dignity was not going to let me ruin that young man life we were in that shit together ad we were getting out of it together.

The new attorney sucked, and I wanted nothing more than to punch him directly in his fucking face. But I needed him, and my court date was quickly approaching, so I had to still be humble and listen to all his lying ass legal bullshit advice. To make a long story short I paid him to keep me out of jail and that's what he did, I took a plea deal for six months probation, no jail time, I had to submit a clean drug test every month and I had to not get any traffic violation during the probationary period.

I argued back and forth with this man about agreeing to that plea deal, I knew it was wrong and did not make any sense, but I wanted all this shit to be over. They wore me down, psychologically tortured me. Promises of leniency, threats of harsher sentences. I cracked, signing a false confession. Tears streamed down my face as I realized what I had done. I had surrendered my freedom, my dignity, to a system designed to crush me.

According to Michelle Alexander in her book "The New Jim Crow" which is one of my personal favorite books I highly recommend that those of you who never read this book do so. She mentions two remarkably interesting points pertaining to my legal situation. She stats "African Americans are 7-10 times more likely to be wrongfully convicted than whites" (p.107) she also stats that "80-90% of criminal cases are resolved through plea bargaining" (p. 92)

My judge was as arrogant as they come, he walked as if the world worshipped him. He knew had the power to change a person's life with one ruling, my competitive nature wanted that smoke from him. I wanted to take this entire case to trail just so I could beat this motherfucker and the system. I knew I could, now you probably asking the question of why did not you. The only reason I did not do so was because I was in the application process to obtain a job in Law Enforcement. Working in law enforcement has always been a childhood dream of mines and I wanted nothing more than to live out that dream.

In court, I witnessed the assembly-line justice system first-hand. Defendants, mostly Black and Latino, paraded before the judge, their fates decided in minutes. The prosecutor's words echoed in my mind: 'You're a drug dealer, a drug user, a menace to society.' I knew I was not alone; many others were falsely accused, coerced into plea deals, or railroaded by the system.

For what it is worth as I scanned the court room, I swear it seemed as if I was in court with a ton of junkies and drug dealers. They appearance did not scream innocent or wrongfully here. I was dressing in a suite and tie along with my codefendant while everyone else was dressed as if they had not been to sleep, showered or just simply clean. I understood why the Judge presented himself the way he did, he viewed everyone as guilty and beneath him.

Looking back, I realize I was just a cog in a machine designed to oppress. A system that prioritizes convictions over justice, perpetuating systemic racism. My story is not unique; countless others suffer the same fate. But I will not be silenced. I'll fight for reform, for equality, and for the freedom to live without fear of false accusation."

My experience taught me that the justice system is broken. It preys on the vulnerable, exploits fear, and destroys lives. But I will not let it break me. I will rise above, using my voice to demand change. We need reform, not just incremental tweaks. We need to address systemic racism, police brutality, and the profit-driven prison industrial complex. We need to humanize those accused, ensuring their rights are protected. No one should endure what I did. No one should fear for their life because of the color of their skin.

Months passed, and my case dragged on. The prosecution's evidence was flimsy, but the damage was done. My reputation was tarnished, my job lost, and my relationships strained. As I walked out of the courtroom, a mix of emotions flooded me: relief, anger, and a deep sadness. I knew I was lucky, but others were not so fortunate.

Years have passed since my ordeal, but the memories linger. I have rebuilt my life, but the scars remain. I share my story, hoping it will inspire change.

STATE OF INDIANA

COUNTY OF STARKE

IN THE KNOX CITY COURT
CONTINUOUS TERM 2016
SITTING AT KNOX, INDIANA

KNOX CITY COURT
MAY 17 2016
FILED

VS

Deangelo Tyler

Cause # 75H01-_1603_-CM-_000266_

PLEA AGREEMENT

The above captioned defendant agrees to plead guilty to the following charges:

Ct 2 Possession of Marijuana (B misd) Discharge   *as conditional*

and enters a conviction to that effect. The Defendant agrees to the following sentence: *dismiss Remaining*

SENTENCE:

_6_ MONTHS IN THE STARKE COUNTY JAIL

_0_ *All stayed* MONTHS OF THAT SENTENCE SUSPENDED

_6_ MONTHS OF NON-REPORTING PROBATION

THE DEFENDANT SHALL PAY:

_____ FINE

_____ RESTITUTION

_$193.⁰⁰_ COURT COSTS

_$200.⁰⁰_ MANDATORY STATE FEES

___ Alcohol Countermeasures
_X_ Drug Interdiction *Stayed*
___ Domestic Violence

DRIVER'S LICENSE SUSPENSION:

_90_ days suspended / _____ days restricted *Stayed*

_____ Complete Defensive Driving

TERMS OF PROBATION:

_X_ Substance Abuse evaluation* *Stayed*

_____ Anger Management / Domestic Abuse counseling*

_____ hours COMMUNITY SERVICE in _____ days**

_X_ Submit to random DRUG SCREENS**

•Do NOT violate any laws
•Do NOT enter any bars or liquor stores
•Do NOT consume or possess alcohol or illegal drugs

_____ OTHER: _______________________

EVALUATION and COUNSELING must be completed / started within 60 days
** *COMMUNITY SERVICE AND DRUG SCREENS must be completed by contacting:* **Starke County Community Corrections, 1911 S. Heaton St., Knox, IN 46534 / Phone: (574) 772-2258**

Court costs, fines, restitution and any other fees must be paid before the defendant is released from probation. If you violate any condition of probation, a petition to revoke probation may be filed before the earlier of the following: within forty-five (45) days of the state finding out about the violation or within one year after the termination of your probation.

I acknowledge by my signature that I have been advised of the terms of my probation and the State's ability to file a petition to revoke my probation should I fail to comply with the Court imposed terms of probation within the above allotted time periods.

_______________________   _______________________   _______________________
DEFENSE ATTORNEY SIGNATURE   DEFENDANT SIGNATURE   STATE PROSECUTOR SIGNATURE

So ORDERED and ADJUDGED this _17_ DAY of _May_, 2016

____
CHARLES F. HASNERL, JUDGE
KNOX CITY COURT

STATE OF INDIANA)   IN THE KNOX CITY COURT
) SS:
COUNTY OF STARKE) CAUSE NO. 75H01-*1603* CM- *000266*

STATE OF INDIANA

  VS   **FILED** CRIMINAL INFORMATION

Deangelo Tyler

  I, the undersigned Affiant, do hereby affirm, under the penalties of perjury, as specified by I.C. 35-44-2-1, that on or about the 29th day of February , 2016, in Starke County the above-captioned defendant did commit:

COUNT: I RECKLESS DRIVING
I.C. 9-21-8-52(a)(1)(A) / CLASS B MISDEMEANOR

____X____ Drive at such an unreasonable (high) (low) rate of speed under the circumstances (as to endanger the safety or property of others), or (as to block the proper flow of traffic).

_________ Pass another vehicle from the rear while (on a slope) or (on a curve) where vision ahead is obstructed for a distance of less than five hundred (500) feet.

_________ Drive in and out of a line of traffic, except as otherwise permitted.

_________ Speed up or refuse to give one-half (1/2) of the roadway to a driver overtaking and desiring to pass.

All of which is contrary to the laws of the State of Indiana and against the peace and dignity thereof.

DATED: March 1, 2016

             Officer Chad Dulin, Knox Police Dept.

STATE'S WITNESSES:

    APPROVED BY: NICHOLAS A. BOURFF
         Prosecuting Attorney
         44th Judicial District

    BY:
    AUTUMN C. FERCH
    Deputy Prosecuting Attorney
    #30228-64

STATE OF INDIANA   )   IN THE KNOX CITY COURT
) SS:
COUNTY OF STARKE   )   CAUSE NO. 75H01-________CM-_____

STATE OF INDIANA

        VS   CRIMINAL INFORMATION

Deangelo Tyler

   I, the undersigned Affiant, do hereby affirm, under the penalties of perjury, as specified by I.C. 35-44-2-1, that on or about the 29 day of February , 2016, in Starke County the above-captioned defendant did commit:

COUNT: II POSSESSION OF MARIJUANA
I.C. 35-48-4-11(a) / CLASS B MISDEMEANOR

A person who knowingly or intentionally possesses (pure or adulterated) marijuana, hash oil, hashish, or salvia; knowingly or intentionally grows or cultivates marijuana; or knowingly that marijuana is growing on the person's premises, fails to destroy the marijuana plants.

All of which is contrary to the laws of the State of Indiana and against the peace and dignity thereof.

DATED: 3-01-2016   SIGNED ___________________________
                              PRINTED: Chad E. Dulin KPD

STATE'S WITNESSES:

                              APPROVED BY: NICHOLAS A. BOURFF
                                    Prosecuting Attorney
                                    44th Judicial District

                              BY: ___________________________
                                  AUTUMN C. FERCH
                                  Deputy Prosecuting Attorney
                                  #30228-64

STATE OF INDIANA)   KNOX CITY COURT
)
COUNTY OF STARKE)   CAUSE NO. 75H01-_____-____-_____

STATE OF INDIANA

           AFFIDAVIT
   VS.   **FOR**

          PROBABLE CAUSE

Deangelo Tyler

I, the undersigned Affiant, do hereby affirm, under the penalties of perjury as specified by I.C. 35-44-2-1, that the foregoing representations are true:

1) I am an officer with the Knox Police Department.

2) I investigated criminal violations involving the above-named Defendant.

3) I prepared a **report** regarding the investigation and arrest of the Defendant. The Defendant was arrested on February 29th, 2016 at 10:50a.m.

4) To the best of my knowledge and belief, the information in the report is true.

5) **The report is attached** as Exhibit A and incorporated herein.

6) The report contains the facts upon which I based my finding that probable cause existed for the arrest of the Defendant for the charge(s) of:

I) Reckless Driving
II) Possession of Marijuana

FURTHER AFFIANT SAITH NOT.

  March 1st, 2016

                Chad E. Dulin
                Knox Police Department

Case 2016-000683 Report

Knox, In
Knox PD
Case Report

Case #: 2016-000683   **Date: 02/29/2016 Time: 10:28**

Event: **Status:** OFC REPORT
Code: 8028 **Description** TRAFFIC STOP
Case Officer: 4406 - C.DULIN2
Source: OFFICER **Condition:** IN PROGRESS
Location:
Address: BP GAS STATION,KNOX, IN,
Contact: KPD:4406
Place Code: RESIDENCE-COMMON
Time:
Occurred From: 02/29/2016 10:28 **To:** 02/29/2016 10:28 **Reported:** 02/29/2016 10:28
Closing Information:
Response: CITATION **Status:** PND **False Alarm:** NA **Date/Time:** 02/29/2016
12:05 **Closed Status:** NO REPORT

02/29/2016 10:28 Badge/Name: 7587/C.RAY
Officer Initiated Traffic Stop

02/29/2016 10:30 Badge/Name: 7586/C.HINSHAW
4406 Status Check - Unit checks OK

02/29/2016 10:33 Badge/Name: 7586/C.HINSHAW
4406 Status Check - Unit checks OK

02/29/2016 10:34 Badge/Name: 7586/C.HINSHAW
44-6 ADVISED 10-6 VEH SEARCH, ALSO ADVISED 75-2 IS 10-23 AS WELL

02/29/2016 10:35 Badge/Name: 7586/C.HINSHAW
4406 Status Check - Unit checks OK

02/29/2016 10:40 Badge/Name: 7586/C.HINSHAW
4406 Status Check - Unit Timer cancelled by operator

02/29/2016 10:40 Badge/Name: 7586/C.HINSHAW
44-6 ADVISED CONTRABAND FOUND, HAVE 2 DETAINED AT THIS TIME /// REQ NO
FURTHER STATUS

02/29/2016 10:47 Badge/Name: 7586/C.HINSHAW

3/1/2016 11:59:11 AM

75-2 10-8

02/29/2016 10:56 Badge: 7586 WSID: D:SCDISPATCH-W
Tow Requested - BUZZ'S /// RANDY ADVISED HE'S UNAVAILABLE /// ADVISED 44-6

02/29/2016 10:56 Badge/Name: 7587/C.RAY
75-3 transporting 1mj3 for 44-6

02/29/2016 10:57 Badge: 7586 WSID: D:SCDISPATCH-W
Tow Requested - HAUSER'S TOWING /// ADVISED 44-6 HAUSER'S WILL BE EN ROUTE

02/29/2016 10:58 Badge/Name: 7587/C.RAY
75-6 TRANSPORTING 1MJ3 FOR 44-6

02/29/2016 10:59 Badge/Name: 7587/C.RAY
75-3 10-23 ON STATION

02/29/2016 11:01 Badge/Name: 7587/C.RAY
75-6 10-23 ON STATION

02/29/2016 11:04 Badge/Name: 7587/C.RAY
44-6 ADVD 10-8 FROM SCENE HAUSERS HAS VEHICLE// 44-6 ENROUTE TO SCSD

02/29/2016 11:10 Badge/Name: 7587/C.RAY
75-3 75-6 10-8

02/29/2016 16:09 Badge/Name: 4406/C.DULIN2

Arrest Report

Deangelo V. Tyler
1.) Reckless Driving
2.) Possession of Marijuana

On the date of February 29th, 2016 at approximately 10:20am, I was running stationary radar at the Knox Train Depot Center facing southbound on US Hwy 35. While monitoring traffic, I observed a dark or black colored vehicle traveling southbound on US Hwy 35 at a high rate of speed. I clocked the vehicle on radar at 57mph in a 35mph posted zone near the intersection of Water St. and US Hwy 35.

At this time, I activated my red and blue emergency lights on my fully marked commission and pursued the vehicle to make a traffic stop. I was able to conduct a traffic stop on the black 2007 Dodge Caliber bearing IL. Temporary plate ▮▮▮▮▮ at the BP gas Station. I radioed dispatch of my location and plate information on the vehicle. I exited my commission wearing full uniform and approached the driver who identified himself with an IL. drivers license as Deangelo Tyler ▮▮▮▮▮ I observed a male front passenger in the vehicle ▮▮▮▮▮ ▮▮▮▮▮ provided me his is IL. drivers license.

I explained to Deangelo the reasoning for the traffic stop. Doing so I detected an odor of burnt marijuana emitting from inside of the vehicle. I radioed Deangelo Tyler's drivers information and a warrants check on ▮▮▮▮▮ to dispatch. Starke County Chief Deputy Ken Pfost arrived on scene to assist. I requested Deangelo to exit the vehicle. I spoke to Deangelo

3/1/2016 11:59:11 AM

Case 2016-000683 Report 4

Contact: KPD:4406

DRIVER, ARRESTED:
Name: TYLER, DEANGELO V
Address: ███████████████████
Place Code: RESIDENCE-COMMON
Details: Sex: M Race: B DOB: ██████ Age: 26 Height: 6' 1" Weight: 198 lbs Hair
Color: BROWN Hair Style: SHORT Facial Hair: PARTIAL BEARD Eye Color: BROWN
Identifiers: DL: ██████ ST: IL
Charge - On: 02/29/2016 00:00 Charged By: 4406 - C.DULIN2 Offense: IC 35-48-4-11(A)
MB ~ POSSESSION OF MARIJUANA/HASH OIL/HASHISH OR SALVIA
Charge - On: 02/29/2016 00:00 Charged By: 4406 - C.DULIN2 Offense: IC 9-21-8-52 ~
RECKLESS DRIVING

ARRESTED:
Name: ███████████████
Address: █████████████████
Place Code: RESIDENCE-COMMON
Details: Sex: M Race: B DOB: ██████ Age: 19 Height: 5' 9" Weight: 164 lbs Hair
Color: BROWN Hair Style: SHORT Eye Color: BROWN
Identifiers: DL: ██████ ST: IL
Charge - On: 02/29/2016 00:00 Charged By: 4406 - C.DULIN2 Offense: IC 35-48-4-11(A)
MB ~ POSSESSION OF MARIJUANA/HASH OIL/HASHISH OR SALVIA

STOPPED:
LIC: █████ ST: IL Type: TM Year: 2016
Make/Model: Type: AUTO Make: DODGE Model: CALIBER Style: HARDTOP
4DR Year: 2007 Color: BLACK

Call Profile:
Race: B Sex: M
NumberOfTickets 1 Reason For Stop: MOVING VIOLATION Reason
Type: SPEED Result of Stop: CITATION Search Requested: No
Vehicle Search: SEARCHED WITHOUT REQUEST NO Consent Search
Performed: No Contraband Found: Yes Contraband Type: DRUGS Drug Amount: 2-10
GRAMS
Driver Search: SEARCHED WITHOUT REQUEST Contraband Found: Yes Contraband
Type: DRUGS Drug Amount: 2-10 GRAMS
Police Dog Sniffed: Yes Police Dog Alerted: Yes Police Dog Caused Search: No
Police Dog Contraband Found: No

Evidence Items		
Item TAG	Property Type Log Date,Time,Badge	Details
1	DRUGS	Make: ASHTRAY Model: GLOW TOP / CUP HOLDER Serial: NA Quantity: 1.00 Description: ASHTRAY GLOW TOP SMOKE-FREE CUP HOLDER STYLE

3/1/2016 11:59:11 AM

Chapter 6

The Enemy Within

I Spent over ten years of working in both law enforcement and social service, I have seen firsthand the harsh realities of the incarceration system. My decade-long tenure has exposed me to the darkest aspects of human nature, testing my resolve and compassion. Correctional officers bear the burden of maintaining order within facilities, ensuring the safety of inmates and colleagues. This weighty responsibility demands unwavering vigilance, as officers navigate volatile environments.

As a rookie officer, I naively embarked on my law enforcement journey, blinded by the promise of a steady paycheck and what I thought would be a stable career. I had no idea what lay ahead - the harsh realities, the dangers, and the emotional toll. I envisioned order and structure but instead found chaos and unpredictability. The gruesome conditions, violent outbursts and ingrained corruption shook me to my core. Every shift became a gamble with my safety, testing my resolve and humanity. Initially lured by financial stability, I soon realized the true cost of wearing the badge.

Fast forward exactly three years later into my career as a

duty sheriff, I experienced a shocking and embarrassing encounter at work. I saw the jailbird being processed into the county jail, and my first reaction was disbelief. His appearance was unrecognizable - disheveled hair, worn-out clothes hanging loosely from his out of shape body. I felt embarrassed, but why?

In retrospect, I realized that my embarrassment stemmed from comparing my father to those of my colleagues. They would proudly share stories about their dads, and some even worked alongside their fathers, showcasing a loving bond I could only dream of.

As I stood there, frozen in shock, I called my mother to confirm my suspicions. After years of absence, I finally had a chance to keep tabs on him. My father avoided eye contact, perhaps sensing my anger and disappointment. I struggled to contain my emotions, fighting the urge to confront him. The professional environment was the only thing that stopped me.

That moment was a painful reminder of our complicated past, and I could not help but wonder what could have been if he had been present in my life. The encounter left me torn between emotions, but it also made me realize that my feelings were valid, and I needed to address them to move forward.

Curiosity got the better of me, and I investigated his offense records. Expecting to see another drug-related case, I was stunned to discover something far more heinous - criminal sexual assault on a child. My mind reeled in horror. What was he thinking? How could he betray a child's trust?

Thoughts of my own children flooded my mind. I had always wanted him to be a loving grandfather to them. Now, I realized that having him in their lives would put them in danger. My stepfather, a man I respected, would never cross those boundaries. He treated me and my brothers with kind-ness and love.

This revelation marked the end of our strained relationship

for me. Any lingering hope for reconciliation vanished. He would finally face the consequences of his actions. No child deserves to lose their innocence to exploitation and abuse.

A mix of emotions swirled within me - anger, disappointment, sadness. I knew he must have been under the influence of drugs when he committed this atrocity. Yet, that was no excuse. His actions were inexcusable.

I remembered predicting this moment, knowing our paths would cross in my line of work. But I never imagined it would be under these circumstances. Fate has a way of revealing truth.

As I processed this new information, my professional demeanor remained intact, but inside, turmoil raged. How could the man who gave me life be capable of such harm? My thoughts turned to the victim and their family. I hoped they found solace in knowing justice would be served. My father's actions demanded accountability. In that moment, I knew I had to prioritize justice over familial bonds. My duty as a sheriff and protector of my community took precedence. This experience forever changed me, leaving scars but also resolve. I vowed to protect innocent lives and ensure perpetrators faced justice. The memory still lingers, a harsh reminder of the darkness that exists, but also of my unwavering commitment to justice and safeguarding those who need protection.

Childhood sexual abuse leaves an indelible mark on victims, profoundly affecting their mental health and well-being. Children often struggle with anxiety, depression, post-traumatic stress disorder, and complex trauma. These issues can manifest immediately or years later, influencing relationships, self-esteem, and daily functioning. For those incarcerated the cumulative effect of incarceration, societal rejection and ongoing stigma can severely impact mental health, increasing anxiety, depression, and suicide risk among sex offenders.

The emotional scars of childhood sexual abuse can lead to self-destructive behaviors, substance abuse, and eating disorders. Victims may also experience dissociation, numbness, or hyperarousal, making everyday interactions challenging. Trust issues and intimacy fears can strain relationships, causing feelings of isolation. Compared to the predictors within prison walls, sex offenders face harsh realities. They are often segregated from the general population for their own safety due to the stigma surrounding their crimes. This separation can lead to isolation, restricting access to rehabilitation programs and educational resources. Correctional facilities implement strict measures to monitor and manage sex offenders. They are typically housed in specialized units with heightened security and surveillance.

Childhood trauma can rewire the brain, altering stress response systems and emotional regulation. This can result in hypervigilance, nightmares, flashbacks, and avoidance behaviors. Survivors may also grapple with shame, guilt, and self-blame, perpetuating a cycle of pain.

Healing requires specialized support, patience, and understanding. Trauma-informed therapies like cognitive-behavioral therapy (CBT), eye movement desensitization and reprocessing (EMDR), and dialectical behavior therapy (DBT) can facilitate recovery. Support groups and advocacy organizations provide crucial resources. Societal awareness and education are vital in preventing abuse and promoting healing.

While incarcerated, sex offenders undergo mandatory counseling and therapy aimed at addressing underlying issues driving their behavior. These programs focus on accountability, empathy development and behavior modification.

As I stand watch, gazing into the eyes of inmates, I am met with an unsettling familiarity. In my imagination saw my jailbird, a repeated offender, mirroring back at me. The same pain, desperation and hopelessness that once haunted his eyes now reflect in theirs. Memories flood my mind of every time I was lucky enough to speak with him and he would tell me how crazy it is being housed inside a correctional institution. My heart aches, recognizing the parallel paths we have walked.

In those eyes, I also see myself. Not as a criminal but as a product of the same ghetto, same life struggles and same background. Our shared experiences forge an unspoken bond. I understand the systemic forces that drove them to this point: poverty, lack of opportunities and cycles of trauma. Empathy swells within me, fueling my determination to make a difference. I realize that, under different circumstance, I could be standing on the other side of those bars had my situation did not get resolved the way it did.

This connection ignites a sense of purpose – to support redemption, break cycles of pain and offer hope where once there seemed none. I strive to provide guidance, rather than mere supervision, recognizing the human potential beyond the inmate's uniform. Every interaction becomes an opportunity to inspire change.

As days turn into years, I see very little transformation from those incarcerated. You would think inmates would rediscover self-worth, enroll in education programs and create new paths for themselves. Mostly all of them at some point just adapt to the environment. Their lack of successes reaffirms my commitment to this challenging yet rewarding work. Though my jailbird struggles continue to shape me, I find solace in helping others escape the cycles that once ensnared him – and nearly claimed me.

Although I can relate to their unfortunate circumstances, I cannot understand how anyone finds comfort being incarcerated. Living units in jails are often plagued by filthy conditions, creating an environment conducive to chaos. Trash litters the floors, overflowing from overflowing bins. The stench of decay and neglect hangs heavy, a constant reminder of the facility's inadequacies. Unclean showers spread diseases, forcing inmates to choose between hygiene and health risks.

Pests infest the unit, scurrying through shadows. Rodents, mice, and cockroaches roam freely, feasting on discarded food. Inmates endure sleepless nights, anxious about potential encounters. These inhumane conditions erode dignity, fueling frustration.

Violence permeates daily life. Daily assaults, fights and stabbings with homemade weapons become alarming norms. Tensions simmer, ignited by territorial disputes or perceived slights. Correctional officers struggle to keep order as understaffing worsens conflicts.

In this volatile atmosphere, inmates and staff face constant danger. Homemade weapons fashioned from everyday objects pose lethal threats. Stabbings occur without warning. Fights erupt spontaneously. The relentless violence wears down inmates' mental resilience, making rehabilitation elusive. Reform demands improved sanitation, increased staffing, and enhanced rehabilitation programs to break this destructive cycle.

Working as a correctional officer, I have grown accustomed to the harsh environment. The constant din of shouting, clang of steel doors and pungent smells blend into a familiar backdrop. My senses numb to the chaos, no longer registering the severity of surroundings. I move through the facility with practiced detachment.

This desensitization seeps into my psyche, making me indifferent to my own confinement. During long shifts, I am locked within the same walls as inmates, yet it does not resonate. My mind does not acknowledge the irony – I am free yet trapped. Comfortable routine replaces awareness.

Strange familiarity breeds tranquility within the sterile, concrete walls. Conversations with inmates become casual exchanges. Shared experiences forge unexpected bonds, blurring lines between guardian and detainee. Emotional defenses rise, shielding me from the grim reality.

Subconsciously, I have begun to feel that this environment is where I belong. The facility's rigid structure provides a twisted sense of security. I have adapted to the controlled chaos, finding solace in predictable routines. Time passes, and self-reflection reveals this phenomenon. How did I grow so comfortable in a place meant to confine? Did years of immersion erase empathy? Or did survival mechanisms kick in? Questions linger, but one truth remains – this environment has become my norm

Often, inmates turn to substance abuse or alcohol addiction to help them move forward with life. The devastating impact of synthetic drugs and homemade alcohol on inmates. Initially, subtle changes emerged: dilated pupils, erratic mood swings and lethargic demeanor. Over time, physical transformations became stark: sunken cheeks, gaunt frames, and sallow complexions. Behavior shifted from defiance to delusions, with paranoia and aggression intensifying. Character dissolution accelerated as addiction took hold. Men and women once filled with hope and resilience now shuffled through days vacant-eyed, lost to substance-induced hazes. The harsh environment amplified these destructive forces, eroding inmates' humanity and leaving hollow shells.

Inmates in county jails are vulnerable to addiction, and prescription medication is often the culprit. These medications, intended to treat legitimate medical conditions, are frequently misused by inmates to get high or make money by selling to other inmates.

The ease of access to prescription medication in county

jails contributes to the problem. Inmates may receive medications for legitimate medical conditions, but they may also find ways to obtain medications from other inmates or even from corrections staff.

Once inmates have access to prescription medication, they may begin to misuse it to get high. Opioids, benzodiazepines, and stimulants are particularly popular among inmates due to their euphoric effects.

Inmates may also use prescription medication to self-medicate for underlying mental health issues, such as anxiety or depression. However, this self-medication can quickly turn into addiction, as inmates become dependent on the medication to cope with their emotions.

The consequences of misusing prescription medication in county jails can be severe. Inmates may experience withdrawal symptoms, such as nausea, vomiting, and tremors, when they are unable to obtain the medication.

Long-term misuse of prescription medication can have devastating effects on a person's mental and physical health. Opioids, for example, can lead to respiratory depression, overdose, and even death.

Benzodiazepines, commonly used to treat anxiety, can lead to cognitive impairment, memory loss, and increased risk of falls and accidents.

Stimulants, such as Ritalin or Adderall, can lead to cardiovascular problems, including heart palpitations, high blood pressure, and stroke.

In addition to the physical health consequences, misusing prescription medication can also have severe mental health consequences. Inmates may experience increased anxiety, depression, and suicidal thoughts.

The effects of misusing prescription medication can be long-lasting, even after inmates are released from jail. Many inmates struggle with addiction and substance abuse long after their release, which can lead to a cycle of recidivism.

Breaking the cycle of addiction requires comprehensive treatment and support. Inmates need access to show-based treatment programs, counseling, and support groups to address their addiction and underlying mental health issues.

Providing inmates with access to these resources can help reduce the risk of overdose, recidivism, and long-term health consequences. By addressing the root causes of addiction and providing support and treatment, we can help inmates overcome their addiction and lead healthier, more productive lives.

Hooch is considered to be the Jailhouse brew. It is a potent, illicit beverage crafted from readily available ingredients within correctional facilities. I have seen or knew this brew or be made several diverse ways but typically the ingredients can be anything. Fruit like apples, oranges, sugar, water, and yeast or bread. For preparation, Inmates combine fruit, sugar, and water in a container, often a plastic bag or bottle.

Yeast or bread is added to start fermentation, which can take several days. The smell is extraordinarily strong and can easily be recognized. Once the shit has settled, the liquid is strained and consumed, often in small quantities due to its potency.

My first time ever knowing this existed was when I was working in a maximum-security prison in Indiana. It was the rapper 2pac birthday i was working the night shift in an extremely dangerous cell house. As the night ended, the inmates just returned from chow hall. We made the announcement for everyone to return to the cells for lockdown. Out of nowhere I saw various inmates running around the cell house passing a clear liquid object in a transparent plastic cup. I stop one inmate and asked his what are y'all drinking that got everybody so excited. He looked me directly in my eyes and said its hooch we are getting drunk for 2Pac birthday. I thought he was joking but after asking a coworker they confirmed.

Unfortunately, some drugs are harder to detect only because by the time you knew it was there it would have been used already. Inmates often turn to synthetic drugs as a coping mechanism within incarceration's harsh environment. These substances, such as K2 or Spice, offer fleeting escapes from reality. Despite strict controls, contraband flows into facilities through various channels.

Synthetic drugs' allure lies in their accessibility and potency. Inmates manufacture or obtain these substances through clandestine networks, exploiting vulnerabilities within facilities. Consumption becomes rampant, fueled by desperation.

Disturbingly, some correctional officers succumb to corruption. They smuggle contraband into facilities, trading substances for bribes or favors. This betrayal compromises security and integrity. The consequences are dire overdoses, violence and addiction intensify. Facilities struggle to have the issue, hampered by limited resources and systemic failures. Reform demands enhanced security measures, officer training and rehabilitation programs addressing addiction's root causes.

Inmates struggling with mental health issues often receive prescription medications to alleviate symptoms. Correctional facilities provide psychiatric services, aiming to rehabilitate and stabilize inmates. However, some inmates exploit this system, seeking medications for illicit purposes. They feign symptoms or manipulate healthcare providers to obtain desirable prescriptions.

Misused medications become commodities within facilities. Inmates trade or sell pills for favors, protection, or currency. This underground market thrives due to lack of effective monitoring and inadequate staffing. The consequences are multifaceted and the addiction spreads, and genuine mental health needs are overshadowed. Facilities must enhance monitoring, improve staffing, and implement effective rehabilitation programs addressing addiction and mental health.

Inmates, desperate for escape or self-medication, mixed mental health medications with jailhouse drugs. This deadly combination intensified addiction. Upon release, they received little to no support or resources to combat their deepening dependence. This systemic failure perpetuated recidivism, fueling a vicious cycle

The correctional system's inaction on substance abuse and addiction undermines its purpose. Rehabilitation requires comprehensive support, including counseling, mental health services, and post-release resources. Until we address these shortcomings, we risk perpetuating a cycle of addiction, harming individuals and communities.

Substance abuse be wreaking havoc on the mind, driving those individuals to erratic behavior. Substances would alter brain chemistry, warping perception, and rational thought. As they addiction intensifies, the inmates became prone to impulsive decisions.

Under the influence, inmate show bizarre behaviors. The common symptoms would be hallucination, paranoia, and disconnection from reality. They may become aggressive, lashing out at others or themselves. In extreme cases, drug-induced psychosis triggers violent outbursts.

The grip of addiction destroys inhibitions, leading them to engage in risky acts. They may compromise personal safety, engage in illicit activities, or harm anyone the encounter. Rational thinking gives way to obsessive cravings.

CHAPTER 7

FADING MEMORIES, FADING POWERS

Why did Grandma bring a ladder to the party?

Because she heard the drinks were on the house!

<u>In Loving Memory of my grandma, Ms. Mary Ann Tyler</u>

"Indeed, we belong to Allah, and indeed to Him we will return."
—Holy   Quran,   Surah   AL-Baqarah, verse 156

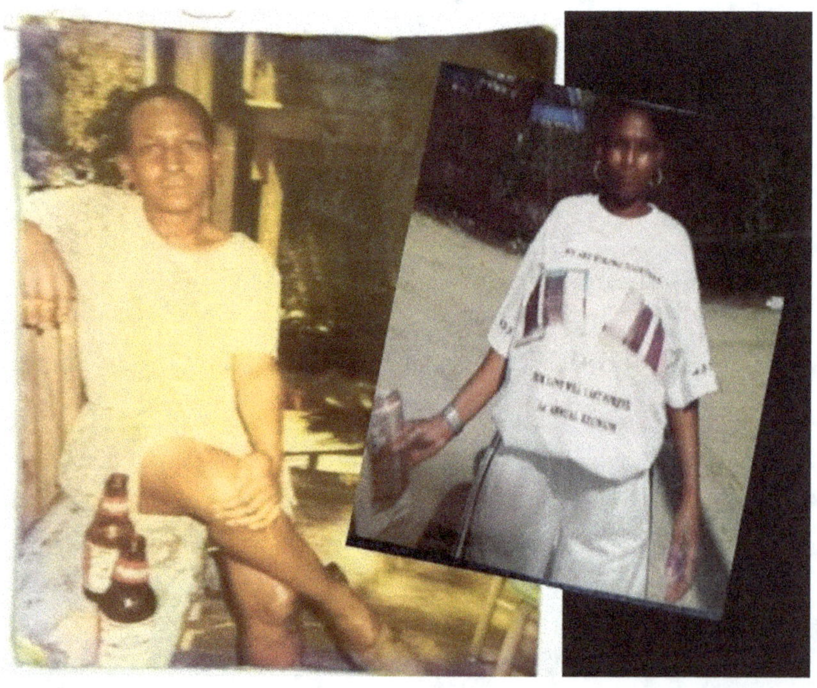

The taste of alcohol is something that has always perplexed me. To me, it is a bitter, acrid flavor that burns my tongue and leaves a lingering unpleasantness in my mouth. I just cannot fathom how anyone could find enjoyment in such a nasty tasting beverage. Whether it is beer, wine, or liquor, the taste of alcohol is something that I have never been able to acquire. Let us not be hypocritical here I have tried several types, thinking that I just had not found the right one yet, but every time I am left with the same reaction: fucking disgusted.

I have always wondered what it is about the taste of alcohol that people enjoy. Is it the way it burns going down? The bitter aftertaste? The way it makes your face contort in discomfort. I just do not get it. To me, drinking alcohol is like intentionally subjecting yourself to an unpleasant experience. And yet, despite my confusion, millions of people around the world enjoy drinking alcohol on a regular basis. I suppose it is just one of those things that I will never understand, but I am happy to stick to my non-alcoholic beverages, thank you very much!

What bothers me the most is when people try to convince me that I am missing some great experience by not drinking. They will say things like, "You just haven't found the right drink yet!" or "It's an acquired taste!" But I am not interested in acquiring a taste for something that I find unpleasant. I would much rather stick to my soda, juice, or water. And I wish others would respect my decision and not try to pressure me into drinking something that I clearly do not enjoy.

In contemporary society, the media plays a significant role in shaping public perceptions of alcohol use. Movies, television shows, and commercials often depict alcohol consumption as a symbol of celebration, sophistication, or a means to escape life's troubles. While these portrayals are entertaining and resonate with cultural norms, they frequently do not convey the true effects of alcohol addiction. This selective representation not only minimizes the gravity of addiction but also perpetuates misconceptions about its impact on individuals and society.

Movies and television shows often glamorize alcohol use, presenting it as a central part of the characters lives. The protagonists are often shown enjoying drinks in social settings, using alcohol as a tool for relaxation, or even as a coping mechanism. For example, characters like Don Draper from Mad

Men or Tony Stark from the Iron Man franchise are portrayed as successful individuals who regularly consume alcohol. Their struggles with addiction, when addressed, are often romanticized or downplayed, not illustrating the long-term physical, emotional, and societal consequences of alcoholism.

Additionally, the media tends to associate alcohol with charm, creativity, or rebellion. This portrayal normalizes excessive drinking, especially for young viewers, and establishes a misleading narrative that consuming alcohol is an integral part of adult life. Rarely are the severe consequences such as liver damage, mental health disorders, or the impact on personal relationships given the same screen time or depth of exploration.

By trivializing these effects, the media reinforces harmful stereotypes and diminishes the reality of alcohol addiction.

Speaking of alcohol commercials, that is another powerful medium through which the effects of alcohol are misrepresented. Marketing campaigns often highlight alcohol as a gateway to fun, friendship, and success. For example, beer advertisements often feature groups of young, attractive individuals enjoying life at parties, beaches, or sports events. Similarly, luxury liquor brands emphasize sophistication, aligning their products with high-status lifestyles.

What these commercials omit are the detrimental health effects associated with excessive alcohol consumption. There is no mention of the risks of addiction, the potential for impaired judgment, or the long-term damage to vital organs. Instead, alcohol is framed as a harmless product that enhances social experiences. By focusing solely on the positive aspects, these advertisements contribute to the normalization of drinking culture and obscure the serious consequences of misuse.

The media's reluctance to address the adverse effects of alcohol stems from both cultural and economic factors. Alcohol companies are among the largest advertisers in the entertainment industry, and their influence often dictates the narrative.

Acknowledging the devastating effects of alcohol addiction would not only disrupt the positive image cultivated by advertisers but might also alienate audiences who prefer escapism over realism.

Furthermore, when the negative effects of alcohol are depicted, they are often sensationalized or used as plot devices rather than explored in a nuanced, educational manner. For instance, characters suffering from alcoholism may face dramatic consequences like losing a job or experiencing a public meltdown, but these portrayals rarely delve into the everyday struggles of addiction, such as withdrawal symptoms, strained family dynamics, or the challenge of seeking help.

The media's skewed portrayal of alcohol use and addiction has far-reaching implications. First, it contributes to the stigmatization of those struggling with addiction. Since movies and TV shows often frame alcoholics as flawed or morally weak, viewers may develop a judgmental attitude toward addiction rather than understanding it as a complex, multifaceted issue. This stigma can deter individuals from seeking help, perpetuating cycles of abuse and denial.

Second, these portrayals influence societal norms, particularly among young audiences. Adolescents and young adults, who are highly impressionable, may internalize the message that drinking is both desirable and without significant risk. This can lead to higher rates of underage drinking, binge drinking, and the eventual development of dependency.

Finally, the lack of transparency about the risks of alcohol use in media perpetuates a public health issue. Alcohol-related illnesses, accidents, and fatalities remain a leading concern worldwide. By not highlighting these consequences, the media misses an opportunity to educate the public and challenge unhealthy cultural norms around alcohol consumption.

I would argue that my grandmothers drink of choice would be a nice cold beer. Since she drank so much of it I mad sure she was aware of all the health related concerns I mean how could she not have been the ingredients are posted on the back of the damn bottle. Before I get into talking about my beloved grandmother. If I may, I wanna share two images with you. The first image represents the facts about the ingredients in inside of my grandmothers favorite beverage. The second image represents the ingredients of what I believe my grandmother was made of after consuming this beverage.

Nutrition Facts

Serving Size: 28g
Servings Per Container About 4

Amount Per Serving
Calories 160   Calories from Fat 100

	% Daily Value*
Total Fat 12g	18%
Saturated Fat 1.5g	7%
Trans Fat 0g	
Cholesterol 0mg	0%
Sodium 60mg	3%
Total Carbohydrate 12g	4%
Dietary Fiber 2g	8%
Sugars 8g	
Protein 3g	

Vitamin A 0%	Vitamin C 0%
Calcium 4%	Iron 4%
Vitamin D 0%	Vitamin E 0%

* Percent Daily Values are based on a 2,000 calorie diet. Your daily values may be higher or lower depending on your calorie needs:

		Calories	2,000	2,500
Total Fat	Less than		65g	80g
Sat Fat	Less than		20g	25g
Cholesterol	Less than		300mg	300mg
Sodium	Less than		2,400mg	2,400mg
Total Carbohydrate			300g	375g
Dietary Fiber			25g	30g

Calories per gram:
Fat 9   ·   Carbohydrate 4   ·   Protein 4

Life in the Robert Taylor housing projects was a constant struggle for survival. My grandmother, had seen it all the poverty, the gangs, the murders, the drugs, and the use of alcohol consumption on the regular. Every day was a battle to provide for her family, to keep them safe from the dangers that lurked around every corner of the project hallways. I am sure my grandmother had memories of the sound of gunfire echoing through the halls, the screams of women and children, and the endless stream of police sirens. Despite the chaos, she tried to create a sense of normalcy for her family, but that task most days seemed unreal.

The Robert Taylor Housing Projects was a sprawling, dilapidated complex of high-rise buildings that seemed to stretch on forever. The exterior walls were a dull, faded brown, covered in graffiti, and cracked, crumbling concrete. Broken windows, some boarded up with plywood, others left gaping open, seemed to stare out like empty eyes. The air was thick with the smells of decay and neglect - the stench of rotting garbage, the acrid tang of smoke from fires set in trash cans, and the sweet, cloying scent of urine that seemed to permeate every corner of the complex. The sounds of the projects were just as overwhelming - the constant wail of sirens, the shouts and screams of arguments, and the thumping bass of music played at ear-shattering decibels.

Despite the bleak surroundings, the people living in the Robert Taylor Housing Projects were a vibrant, resilient community. Mothers, grandmothers, and great-grandmothers, worn down by years of struggle, sat on stoops, watching over their children and grandchildren with a fierce, protective love. Young men, some with faces already hardened by the streets, others still soft with the promise of youth, congregated on corners, laughing, joking, and posturing. Children, their eyes wide with wonder, played in the crumbling courtyards, their laughter and shouts a defiant rebuke to the bleakness that surrounded them. Everywhere, there was a sense of community, of people looking out for one another, of a shared struggle against the poverty, violence, and neglect that threatened to consume them. Despite the many challenges they faced.

The stress of living in such a harsh environment took a toll on her mental and physical health. Due to this, my grandmother often found herself anxious and on edge, never knowing when the next violent outbreak would occur. The constant fear of losing a loved one to the streets was a weight that she carried with her every day. This I know because my grandmother expressed this to me when I asked her what her life was like. To cope with the stress, she turned to substances, seeking temporary relief from the pain and anxiety. At first, it was just a drink or two to calm her nerves, but soon she found herself relying on alcohol to get through the day. The addiction crept up on her, slowly but surely, until she was trapped in a cycle of dependence.

My grandmother's smile would illuminate any room, but behind her warm eyes, a secret sorrow lingered. Between her groovy dance moves and innocent stare at the television when she would watch Tyler Perry movies, I saw that sorrow in her eyes. For years, she used alcohol to numb the pains of her past, to silence the whispers of her inner critic and to cope with many family deaths and her weight of responsibilities as the head of the family. But as the bottles emptied, her health began to decline, I watched in helpless horror as she slipped away, one sip at a time.

As I reflect on her journey, I realize that my grandmother's story is a testament to the destructive power of alcohol addiction and the resilience of the human spirit. Follow me as I explore the early warnings signs of her alcohol addiction, my family dynamics that enabled her habits, and the devastating consequences that followed. Since my grandmother is no longer here to explain and narrate her own story, I am positive she would be proud and grateful that her grandson found her life to be an impression to get out and help others over come substance abuse and alcohol addiction.

As the years went by, the grandmother's addiction worsened, and she began to struggle with other substances as well. The drugs and alcohol became a way for her to escape the reality of her situation, to temporarily forget the trauma and pain that she had endured. But the escape was short-lived, and the consequences of her addiction were severe. She lost relationships with her family members, struggled to make ends meet, and even found herself in physical altercations with others. The cycle of addiction had taken hold, and it seemed impossible to break free.

Despite the darkness that surrounded her, my grandmother held on to the hope that things could get better. She knew that she was not alone in her struggles, that there were others out there who were fighting the same battles. I never asked her if she ever tried to seek help, like attending support groups and counseling sessions to help her slowly but surely rebuild her life. If I had to guess I would say because I am sure It was not easy to do so during that time in her life. There were many setbacks along the way, but she refused to give up.

According to the World Health Organization, approximately 270 million people suffering from substance use disorders, with 140 million struggling with alcohol addiction. Substance abuse and alcohol addiction are pervasive issues affecting individuals, families, and communities worldwide. These destructive disorders know no boundaries, transcending geographical, cultural, and socioeconomic lines.

Between me and you, when drunk my grandmother could have kicked anyone ass. Losing my grandmother has broken me in some many pieces and truthfully speaking I am forever broken. I remember the sound of my grandmother's laughter, the way she would call my name when she would see me, I remember the way her eyes sparkled when she told stories and complained about things. But I also remember the sound of beer cans being crunch up, the smell of beer on her breath, and the silence that followed. For years, my family tiptoed around her addiction, afraid to confront the elephant in the room until it was too late.

My grandmother's most vivid memories are etched in my mind, showcasing her vibrant spirit and unconditional love. Despite her struggles with alcohol, those moments are still dear to me. Honestly, I had the most fun during her drunkest and darkest moments.

When she had a drink her infectious spirit and apex

predator nature would shine. When I would visit her the living room would transform into a wrestling arena, with Grandma taking on my siblings, cousins, friends, and me. Her energy was unmatched, and we cherished those carefree moments. We never defeated her as she remains the heavyweight champion.

She would often take those playful moments to the extreme. One unforgettable afternoon my two brothers and our heavy-set neighbor engaged in playful wrestling on our back porch. The dynamics suddenly shifted when my intoxicated grandmother stumbled out and joined the fray. To our astonishment, she grasped our neighbor and delivered a devastating body slam over the banister! My brothers and I watched in disbelief as he crashed to the ground, motionless and covered in dirt. We feared the worst, thinking he might be severely injured or worse. But remarkably, he eventually stood up shaken yet intact. Today, that incident remains a hilarious memory we often revisited as we laugh together.

Despite the fun times there was some rough scary time that took place. New Year's Eve was supposed to be a night of celebration, but for me, it is etched in memory as a traumatic evening. As a little boy, I recall my mother sending my siblings and I to our grandmother's house while she went out to revel in the festivities. Unbeknownst to us, that decision would expose us to a harrowing experience.

Upon arrival, we found our grandmother still recovering from the recent birth of my toddler auntie. However, her fragile state was worsened by intoxication, which fueled her volatility. Her boyfriend was present, trying to calm her down, but his efforts were met with resistance. The tension escalated, culminating in an intense argument between the two.

Chaos erupted when my grandmother grasped a champagne bottle and hurled it at her boyfriend. He dodged, but unfortunately, my innocent auntie bore the brunt, suffering a severe facial injury that would leave a lasting scar. Witnessing this horrific incident filled me with sorrow and empathy for my aunt, who did not deserve such trauma.

The aftermath was equally distressing. Police arrived, corralling us into a paddy wagon and taking us to the station. We were handcuffed to a bench, treated like criminals, and left alone in a cold room. Our parents eventually arrived, but the image of my mother's fury – her anger radiating like smoke from her ears and nostrils – remains vivid. That night's events left an indelible mark, shaping my perception of the world's complexities and fragilities. Her drunken anger was uncontrollable and unstable.

One unforgettable afternoon, my two brothers, our heavyset neighbor and I engaged in playful wrestling on our back porch. But the dynamics suddenly shifted when my intoxicated grandmother stumbled out and joined the fray. To our astonishment, she grasped our neighbor and delivered a devastating body slam over the banister! My brothers and I watched in disbelief as he crashed to the ground, motionless and covered in dirt. We feared the worst, thinking he might be severely injured or worse. But remarkably, he eventually stood up, shaken yet intact. Today, that incident remains a hilarious memory, often revisited, and retold with laughter.

At family gatherings, Grandma would outshine everyone on the dance floor. Her moves were effortless, and her passion was contagious. We would watch in awe as she twirled and spun, her joy radiating throughout the room.

Grandma's love knew no bounds. She would fearlessly defend anyone she cared about, standing up to those who dared test her loved ones. Her courage inspired me, and I knew I had a guardian angel in her.

However, as time passed, I know my family had to start growing concerns about Grandma's drinking. They would try to avoid inviting her to function or find excuses for her not to attend. The tension was palpable, and I sensed their frustration and embarrassment.

Despite this, Grandma knew she could count on me. Whenever she could not secure a ride to a family event, she would call me, and I would be there in a heartbeat. I could not resist her charming smile and persuasive tone I will make a deal with her every time by telling her if I get you Grandma you gotta spend the night with me and she always agreed.

Those moments taught me the value of unconditional love and acceptance. Grandma's flaws did not define her; her love, resilience and spirit did. I cherished our bond and the lessons she imparted.

Though her struggles were real, I choose to remember the vibrant, loving grandmother who brought joy to our lives. Her legacy lives on through me, reminding me to embrace life's imperfections and love unconditionally.

One vivid memory of my grandmother is still etched in my mind, a poignant moment that has stayed with me since childhood. It was a doctor's visit, and I was just a young boy going with her.

As we sat in the examination room with her, the doctor delivered his prognosis and instructions to my grandmother. Then, turning to me, he said, "If you ever see your grandmother smoking or drinking, take it away from her." His words struck a chord deep within me.

My grandmother's reaction was unforgettable. Her eyes locked onto mine, conveying a thousand words without speaking one. In that instant, I sensed her thinking, "Dear, you." That silent warning has still been with me forever.

After my grandmother passed away, that memory resurfaced, and I could not shake it off. Similar to the guilt I felt after my cousin's tragic death, this memory brought a crushing sense of responsibility. I fucking failed her I will never forgive myself for letting that doctor down in order to save my grandmother.

I could not help but wonder if I could have done more to protect her. The doctor's words echoed in my mind: "Take it away from her." Could I have prevented her struggles with smoking and drinking?

That moment in the doctor's office became a turning point in my understanding of my grandmother's challenges. Her eyes still haunt me, reminding me of the unspoken words and unresolved emotions.

Alcohol addiction is a significant health issue affecting senior citizens, posing substantial risks to their physical and mental well-being. As people age, their bodies undergo changes that make them more susceptible to the harmful effects of

Senior citizens may turn to alcohol due to various factors, including social isolation, loneliness, chronic pain, anxiety, depression, and grief. Additionally, significant life events like retirement or the loss of a loved one can contribute to substance use.

Alarming statistics highlight the prevalence of alcohol addiction among seniors. Approximately 2.5 million older adults in the United States struggle with substance use disorders. 14% of seniors report binge drinking while Substance abuse among seniors is projected to increase by 150% by 2025.

Alcohol consumption exacerbates age-related health issues such as but not limited to; Liver disease, Cognitive impairment, Increased risk of falls, Interactions with medications and worsening mental health conditions. In addition to, some common triggers that can also provoke the use of alcohol consumption or substance abuse in seniors are retirement, loss of a loved one, health issues, cognitive decline, and trauma. Sometime, identifying alcohol addiction in seniors can be difficult because symptoms can be mistaken for age related issues or social stigma sometimes can prevent them from seeking help or treatment which often have limited access.

My grandmother's struggles with alcohol addiction may have stemmed from unresolved grief and trauma. Losing her parents, siblings, and loved ones could have created a profound sense of loss, triggering a lifelong struggle. The cumulative pain of these losses may have been overwhelming, leading her to seek solace in alcohol.

Losing her parents, siblings and loved ones likely created a profound sense of loss, triggering a lifelong struggle. The cumulative pain of these losses may have been overwhelming, leading her to seek solace in alcohol. Grief can manifest differently in individuals, and for my grandmother, alcohol might have become a coping mechanism.

Unaddressed traumatic experiences may have also contributed to her addiction. Perhaps she harbored secrets, keeping painful memories hidden from our family. Alcohol might have become her coping mechanism, providing temporary escape from haunting memories.

The impact of traumatic events can persist, influencing behavior and mental health. My grandmother's experiences, though unknown to us, could have shaped her relationship with alcohol. Understanding this possibility encourages empathy and compassion.

My grandmother's story is etched in my memory, a testament to the human spirit's ability for transformation. A seven-year hospitalization, precipitated by poor health choices, notably her struggles with alcohol, became a transformative experience. Though her path was fraught with challenges, she appeared stronger, inspiring our family with her resilience.

Alcohol had become an integral part of my grandmother's life, a coping mechanism for life's trials. However, this reliance soon spiraled out of control, wreaking havoc on her physical and mental well-being. The consequences of her choices began to manifest, and her health started to deteriorate rapidly.

The day my grandmother was hospitalized marked a turning point. Seven years would pass before she would stop fighting, a period filled with struggles, setbacks, and moments of clarity. Her hospital room became a sanctuary, a place where she confronted her demons.

The day I learned my grandmother was paralyzed from the waist down, my world crumbled. The energetic woman I knew, whose legs carried her confidently through life, was now confined. Her legs were more than just a part of her body; they symbolized strength, independence, and joy.

I worship the ground my grandmother walked on and now there would be no more footsteps to guide us they all now would be erased by track marks from a wheelchair tire. Grandma steps was laid down gracefully and carefree just like she wanted them to be. When she would get intoxicated, I remember days when I saw her feet shoeless the bottom of her feet covered in dirt from the streets looking on the bright side, she would have no choice but to have clean feet now. Her legs carried her to the store, where she would share laughter with neighbors. Most importantly, they stood firm ten toes down when defending our family, a pillar of resilience. The thought of her in a wheelchair was unbearable.

Life seemed irreparably altered. The image of Grandma radiant smile and energetic movements now contrasted with the harsh reality of her paralysis. Grief overwhelmed me, as I struggled to accept this new chapter. How would she cope? How would we adapt? The uncertainty hung like a shadow, casting doubt on our family's future. I never heard grandma complain one time, she made it work, and she still was ready to "roll out" as she would say.

Seniors living in nursing homes or rehabilitation facilities face elevated risks, including death, depression, loneliness, and various health issues. According to the Centers for Disease Control and Prevention (CDC), approximately 1.4 million residents live in nursing homes , where they are more susceptible to infections, falls and medication errors. The confined environment and lack of social interaction worsen feelings of loneliness and isolation.

Depression affects nearly fifty percent of nursing home residents, significantly affecting mental health. Factors contributing to depression include separation from family, loss of independence and inadequate social support. Loneliness plagues many seniors in institutional care, with 60% reporting feelings of isolation. Social isolation increases mortality risk by 26% and hospitalization risk by 32%.

Seniors in nursing homes are vulnerable to abuse and neglect. The National Center on Elder Abuse reports approximately 1 in 10 seniors experience abuse annually. Types of abuse include physical (29%), emotional (21%) and financial exploitation (14%). Neglect affects 57% of nursing home residents. These alarming statistics underscore the need for vigilant oversight.

Health issues abound in nursing homes, with residents being more prone to falls (734,000 annually), pressure ulcers (60,000-80,000 annually) and infections (1.6-3.8 million annually). Rehabilitation facilities also face challenges, such as medication errors and inadequate staffing ratios. These risks underscore the importance of comprehensive care.

During her prolonged stay, my family documented her journey through photographs. These images, though poignant, told a story of having a warrior spirit. They captured moments of despair but also glimpses of hope. Each photo served as a reminder that even amidst darkness, there is always a way forward. Yet, for me, those photos have become a painful reminder, eclipsing memories of her strength and vitality. I hated social media; I could never log in without seeing her hospitalized or a scary update being posted. Now every time I think of her; I only see her in that seven-year period. All those photos of her in the hospital have wiped away just about every memory I have saved of my grandmother. Sometimes I want to think about her, but I cannot because I can not see past all the pictures of her weak. I never took a picture of my grandmother in that state because I knew that was not her.

Visiting my grandmother was a struggle. Witnessing the strongest and toughest person I knew reduced to a state of weakness and hopelessness was heartbreaking. Feelings of helplessness overwhelmed me; there seemed to be nothing I could do. This experience taught me a valuable lesson: prioritize your health journey.

My grandmother's physical presence was defined by fragility yet belied a profound inner strength. Standing significantly shorter than me, she seemed almost petite, her delicate frame a stark contrast to the immense impact she had on our family. Her short, almost bald hair framed always made me laugh but it also made me question why would sh cut off her hair, I never asked her, but I thought about that every time I saw her. Every time I visited her it was for brief moments, she always wanted me to give her a haircut as she would say "cut it all off."

In her presence, I felt protected and humbled. Towering over her, I was reminded of the contrasts that defined her. Watching her go through life the way she did encourage me to watch what I complained about.

Despite her fragile state, my grandmother's edge, spirit, and heart remained unbroken. Her title as my grandmother was never diminished. She continued to inspire, even in her darkest moments.

As my grandmother laid in her hospital bed, I am sure she may have reflected on her life choices, wondering how alcohol had become such a dominant force. Perhaps she thought about the first reasons she turned to drinking, seeking escape from stress, anxiety, or trauma. Did she ever want to stop? Likely, yes. Addiction's grip can be relentless. Now let us be clear alcohol was not what internally hospitalized her, but it played an excessively significant role in her health.

In quieter moments, my grandmother might have pondered what would have happened if her health had not failed her. Would she have continued down the path of alcohol addiction, or would she have found the strength to quit? Maybe she realized that alcohol had become a coping mechanism, masking deeper pain. Her hospitalization served as a wake-up call for not just her but for me as well.

As she navigated the challenges of recovery, my grandmother possibly realized that stopping was not just about quitting alcohol but confronting underlying health issues. Did she regret her choices? Perhaps. Yet, her journey toward sobriety showed remarkable determination. Her story serves as a testament to the human ability for growth, forgiveness, and redemption, inspiring our family to prioritize health and well-being.

During her seven-year hospitalization, my grandmother faced multiple near-death experiences. Her illness, though stabilized, was silently worsening. Each narrow escape left our family on edge, wondering if she would overcome.

There were times when doctors warned us to prepare for the worst. My grandmother's vital signs would plummet, and medical teams rushed to see about her. Yet, she clung to life.

Despite these daunting ordeals, my grandmother refused to surrender. Her spirit, though weakened, remained unbroken.

She drew strength from loved ones. One fateful night, my grandmother's condition took a turn. Doctors said it was her last chance. But she rallied.

That moment sparked a transformation. My grandmother began focusing on recovery, determined to reclaim her life. My grandmother would occasionally visit home from the rehabilitation facility. My family and I would cherish those moments. During holidays and birthdays, she would return only if her health had improved. She brought warmth, joy, and hope. Her presence ignited laughter and smiles, and for brief periods, we forgot about her struggles. This my grandmother would be the positive life of the party and for once everyone wanted to be around her. We thought she was on the mend, and our hopes soared, grandma became confident in her ability to recover.

Those visits were filled with love, laughter, and reunions. Our home transformed into a haven of happiness as we shared stories, memories, and meals together. Grandma radiant smile lit up the room, reassuring us she was getting better. I savored every moment, clinging to the illusion of normalcy.

However, her departures were always bittersweet. When it was time for her to return to the rehabilitation facility, sadness descended. I did not want her to leave, fearing the struggles she would face. Her reluctance to go back was palpable, and our hearts ached knowing she dreaded the confinement and rigors of treatment.

One of my favorite quotes is by the late grate Marcus Garvey "if you have no confidence in self, you are twice defeated in the race of life." I would argue that if my grandmother did not have a dedicated support system the way she did, her life would have ended sooner.

The unexpected passing of my grandmother left an indelible mark on my family and I, forever placing a profound void in our lives. After seven years of sobriety, her health began to fail, and she slipped away, leaving us in shock, grief, and bewilderment.

My grandmother's journey with alcohol addiction and other underlying health conditions had been long and arduous, marked by periods of darkness and despair. Yet, her unwavering determination and will to win inspired hope within our family. Her triumph over alcohol addiction served as a beacon, illuminating the possibility of redemption and healing.

The news of her passing spread like wildfire, engulfing my family in anguish. My mother and her siblings were particularly devastated, their pain palpable and heart-wrenching. Tears flowed uncontrollably as they grappled with the sudden loss. Their sorrow echoed through our home; a haunting reminder of the void left by her departure.

When I received the news, I was numb, thoughtless, and confused, my stare blank and unresponsive. Time seemed to stand still as my mind struggled to understand the reality. The first shock gave way to overwhelming sorrow, and the weight of grief settled upon me.

Attending her funeral, I typically found solace in numbness when facing death. However, this time my eyes drowned in tears, and my heart felt still, as if it had forgotten its purpose. I just could not process what I was seeing the love of my life laying in a coffin lifeless never to return again. We always never get life or the reason for it until some part of that gets taken away fro us. I have no regrets in life, but I was not there for my grandmother the way I knew she would have been for me. For me, every look in the mirror became a reminder of that.

At the graveyard, watching her body being lowered into the earth, I felt rooted to the spot. Leaving her behind seemed impossible, letting go was the hardest part. Even though I knew it was over I still believed I could have saved her. Once the burial ceremony was over, I watched as everyone walked away turning their back on what I thought was a job not yet finished. Her death spoke to me and before I left her presence, I made a promise to her that I would return back to pay my respect until I completed my journey.

Before her death I talked to my grandmother about traveling the world and helping people, I told her I did not know what or how I was going to do that but that is what I needed to do. I promised her I would take her with me and surprisingly she agreed. She was always the first person I called when I landed in a different country or state that was her moment to live vicariously through me.

Returning home from the funeral, my thoughts swirled in anguish. Yet, amidst grief, a vision appeared: bringing awareness to alcohol addiction, substance abuse and re-entry. This epiphany sparked a resolve within me, illuminating a path forward. I knew this was her wish for me. I was nervous to set out on a journey that seemed impossible, but I had to have the spirit of her. Since her death I been working secretly to complete this task to someday come back to her grave sit and tell her how many lives I have help save and because of her family are still together. I only started my journey in secret because I did not and do not want any to get in the way of the vision my grandmother had for me and disrupt the promise I made to her.

CHAPTER 8

HERO MODE: ACTIVATED

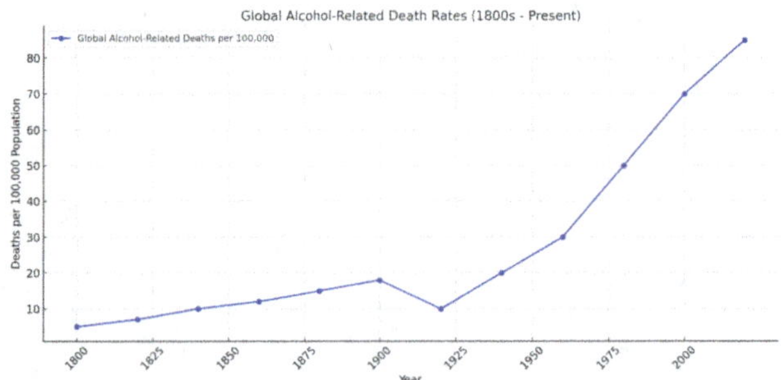

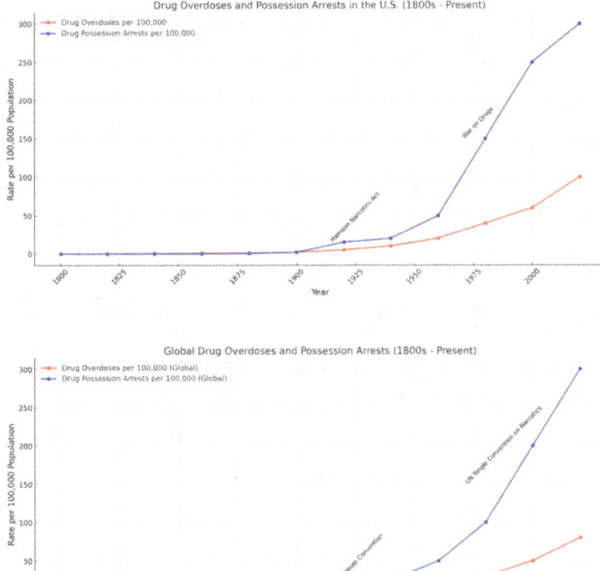

Substance abuse and alcohol addiction have plagued humanity for thousands of years, affecting individuals, families, and communities worldwide. If I may, I want to delve into the history of substance and alcohol abuse, also I want to investigate how substance abuse and alcohol addiction in the United States compare to the rest of the world and highlight the disproportionate impact on underserved communities versus privilege communities.

Evidence of substance use dates to ancient civilizations with alcohol usage dating back even further. In Mesopotamia, around 3000 BCE, opium was used for medicinal and spiritual purposes. Similarly, cannabis was used in ancient China (2737 BCE) and alcohol in ancient Egypt (2500 BCE) and Greece (500 BCE). These substances were initially used for therapeutic and spiritual purposes but eventually became recreational.

During the Middle Ages, substance use spread through

trade routes, introducing opium to China and Europe. Hashish appeared in the Middle East and North Africa, while absinthe gained popularity in Europe. The Industrial Revolution transformed substance use, with mass production and distribution leading to widespread availability. The Opium Wars introduced opiates to China, fueling addiction.

The 20th century saw significant increases in substance abuse, particularly during the 1960s and 1970s. The crack epidemic of the 1980s ravaged urban communities, while prescription opioids became a gateway to addiction in the 1990s and 2000s. Today, synthetic substances like fentanyl contribute to the ongoing opioid crisis.

Substance abuse and alcohol addiction continue to devastate communities worldwide. According to the WHO, over thirty-five million people suffer from substance use disorders. Effective solutions require addressing systemic issues, increasing funding for treatment and prevention, and fostering global cooperation. By understanding the history of substance abuse and addiction, we can develop targeted strategies to mitigate its impact.

The Industrial Revolution brought mass production and distribution of substances, exacerbating addiction rates. The Opium Wars (1839-1842, 1856-1860) introduced opiates to China, while Prohibition (1920-1933) in the United States fueled organized crime and underground substance trade. The 1960s and 1970s saw increased substance use, particularly among youth. The 1980s crack epidemic ravaged urban communities, while prescription opioids became a gateway to addiction in the 1990s and 2000s.

Substance abuse and alcohol addiction have ravaged communities worldwide, leaving irreparable damage. This crisis has escalated into a global pandemic, claiming countless lives and shattering families.

In 2020, approximately 270 million people which is roughly thirteen percent of the global population used illicit drugs. Substance abuse and addiction kill over 200,000 people annually. Alcohol addiction contributes to three million deaths which is fiver percent of global mortality each year. The economic burden of substance abuse exceeds one trillion dollars annually in the United States alone.

Unfortunately, the United States has one of the highest substance abuse rates worldwide. Sadly, the United States accounts for twenty five percent of all global overdose deaths. Despite these alarming statistics, governments worldwide struggle to effectively address this crisis. Insufficient funding, inadequate treatment options and lack of prevention programs exacerbate the issue.

In the United States, only ten percent of individuals struggling with addiction receive treatment. Globally, eighty percent of those needing treatment lack access. Substance abuse disproportionally affects underserved communities. One could argue this statement but if you come from where I am from just step outside and look around the advance is clear. In property-stricken areas residents lack access to healthcare, treatment, and support services. Trauma and systemic racism worsen substance abuse rates amongst minorities. In addition to, the lack of economical opportunities and education the cycles continue.

Here is another statistic I found to be very mind blowing. Since 2020 over forty five percent of African American youth has reported substance abuse. Native Americans communities have experienced a much higher rate of substance abuse and overdose. Lastly, Hispanic and Latinos face barriers to treatment due to the language and culture gaps.

Although, this crisis is unbelievably bad here in America. When comparing these statistics to the rest of the world internationally the problem still continues. In Europe twenty two percent of Europeans suffer a lifetime prevalence of substance abuse disorders. In Australia sixteen percent of individuals have been reported using illicit substance. Canada ten percent of individuals struggled with substance use disorders in 2017.

The consequences of substance abuse and addiction are particularly devastating for children. In the United States, over eight million children live with a substance-abusing parent. Substance abuse and addiction contribute to forty percent of child neglect cases, children of addicted parents face increased risk of emotional trauma, neglect, abuse, abandonment, bulling, and juvenile delinquency.

To combat this crisis, comprehensive approaches are necessary we need to increased funding for treatment and prevention programs, expanded access to education and support service, community-based initiatives promoting healthy coping mechanisms and Policies to help reform addressing root causes.

Growing up, my friends and I would often taunt, prank, and make fun of the neighborhood junkies. We saw them as outsiders, weak and flawed. But little did we understand the grip of addiction. Junkies use to be the target pray for our foolish and immature mentality, on days like Halloween they would become a victim to a full carton of relentless egg throwing. Shit, depending on the day and the crew I have seen some of my friends just walk up and punch the ass directly in the face. I know that harsh but to us as kids that shit was the high light of the day.

One thing for sure, we depended on the junkies to come trough for us. For example, if we needed anything that we could not get personally guess who we counted on, yep, the same junkies we targeted. Truthfully, I do not even know why we found them that interesting enough in the first place. Now that I am older, I remember looking into their eyes and nothing was there, but they were some of the friendliest and nicest people I ever met. Although we did not truest them but benefited tremendously from them.

I wonder if anyone ever viewed my father that way. Nonetheless, substance abuse and alcohol addiction are destructive forces that ravage lives, reputations, and families. They creep in silently, masquerading as temporary escapes, only to ensnare victims in cycles of dependence. For those junkies, addiction stole their dignity, leaving individuals vulnerable to exploitation and manipulation. It destroyed their relationships, eroding trust, and love. Most of the junkies I came encounter with suffered from the consequences of their lifestyle with health problems, organ damage, infections, and cognitive impairment, financial ruin, depleted savings, lost jobs, and debt, legal troubles, arrests, incarceration, and severed ties, social isolation, estrangement from loved ones and the community. It is sick to know I found laughter and joy from adding an ass whooping to their pain.

Have we forgotten that addiction is a disease, not a choice. We overlook the complexities of mental health, trauma, and environment that contribute to substance abuse. Did we ever stop to think what was they life like before the drugs and alcohol? Did we ever care enough to ask them were they ok? Society often views those struggling with addiction as failures, morally flawed, and weak-willed. This stigma perpetuates shame, silence, and suffering.

Despite participating in bullying, I felt a pang of compassion for the junkies. I saw the desperation in their eyes, the plea for help. I wanted to understand their struggles.

As I grew older, my empathy deepened. I realized that addiction was not just a personal issue but a societal problem. We need to address root causes, provide support and resources.

I recognize the harm caused by bullying and disrespect. I

understand now that addiction demands compassion, not ridicule. After losing my grandmother I had to educate myself on addiction and mental health. I had to start offering support to rehabilitation and treatment initiatives. I am now an Advocate for policy changes addressing addiction. I embrace my empathy and understanding and to those junkies I slap upside they head just for fun or made them steal out the corner store for me I am sorry.

The concept of halfway houses and sober living houses has its roots in the late 19th and early 20th centuries. During this time, the United States was experiencing a significant increase in the number of people struggling with addiction, particularly with alcohol (White, 1998). In response to this growing problem, a number of organizations and individuals began to establish facilities that provided a supportive and structured environment for individuals recovering from addiction.

One of the earliest examples of a halfway house was the Salvation Army's "Rescue Homes," which were showed in the late 19th century (Taiz, 2009). These homes provided a safe and supportive environment for individuals recovering from addiction, as well as those who were homeless or struggling with poverty. The Salvation Army's Rescue Homes were based on a model of care that emphasized the importance of spiritual growth, hard work, and community support.

In the early 20th century, the concept of halfway houses continued to evolve, with the establishment of organizations such as the Oxford Group and Alcoholics Anonymous (AA). These organizations provided a supportive community and a structured program of recovery for individuals struggling with addiction. The Oxford Group and AA also emphasized the importance of spiritual growth and personal responsibility in the recovery process.

The modern concept of sober living houses appeared in the

1960s and 1970s, particularly in California. Sober living houses were designed to provide a supportive and structured environment for individuals recovering from addiction, with a focus on peer support and community involvement. Sober living houses were often established in residential neighborhoods and provided a safe and supportive environment for individuals to live and recover.

In the 1980s and 1990s, the concept of halfway houses and sober living houses continued to evolve, with the establishment of new organizations and facilities. This period also saw the emergence of new treatment approaches, such as cognitive-behavioral therapy (CBT) and motivational interviewing (MI). These approaches emphasized the importance of personal responsibility and motivation in the recovery process.

Today, halfway houses and sober living houses can be found in communities all around the world. These facilities provide a critical support system for individuals recovering from addiction and offer a safe and structured environment for individuals to live and recover. Halfway houses and sober living houses also provide a range of services, including counseling, peer support, and job training.

The importance of halfway houses and sober living houses cannot be overstated. These facilities provide a critical support system for individuals recovering from addiction and offer a safe and structured environment for individuals to live and recover. By providing a supportive community and a range of services, halfway houses and sober living houses help individuals to achieve and maintain sobriety, and to rebuild their lives.

Despite the growth and evolution of halfway houses and sober living houses, there is still a significant need for these types of facilities. Many communities lack access to affordable and supportive housing for individuals recovering from addiction, and there is often a shortage of funding and resources to support these facilities.

Substance abuse and alcohol addiction are major contributors to homelessness all around the world. According to the National Coalition for the Homeless, substance abuse is a primary cause of homelessness for many individuals. In the United States, for example, it is estimated that up to 50% of homeless individuals struggle with substance abuse or addiction.

The link between substance abuse, alcohol addiction, and homelessness is complex and multifaceted. One of the primary factors is the cost of substance abuse and addiction. Individuals who struggle with addiction often spend a significant portion of their income on substances, leaving them with limited resources to pay for housing and other basic needs.

Another factor is the impact of substance abuse and addiction on mental and physical health. Individuals who struggle with addiction are more likely to experience mental health problems, such as depression and anxiety, as well as physical health problems, such as liver disease and cardiovascular disease. These health problems can make it difficult for individuals to maintain employment and housing, leading to homelessness.

In addition, substance abuse and addiction can also lead to social isolation and disconnection from family and friends. This social isolation can make it difficult for individuals to access support and resources, leading to homelessness. Furthermore, the stigma surrounding addiction can also make it difficult for individuals to seek help and access.

The link between substance abuse and mental health illness is complex and bidirectional. Individuals who struggle with substance abuse are more likely to experience mental health problems, such as depression and anxiety, as well as personality disorders and psychosis. Conversely, individuals who struggle with mental health problems are more likely to develop substance use disorders as a way of self-medicating or coping with their symptoms. This can create a vicious cycle, where substance abuse worsens mental health problems, and mental health problems increase the risk of substance abuse.

The consequences of this cycle can be severe. Individuals who struggle with co-occurring substance use and mental health disorders are more likely to experience incarceration, homelessness, and death. In fact, individuals with co-occurring disorders are more likely to be incarcerated than those with either substance use or mental health disorders alone. This is often due to the fact that individuals with co-occurring disorders are more likely to engage in high-risk behaviors, such as crime and violence, as a result of their substance use and mental health symptoms.

Incarceration can have devastating consequences for individuals with co-occurring substance use and mental health disorders. Jails and prisons often lack adequate resources and treatment options for individuals with these disorders, leading to a worsening of symptoms and an increased risk of recidivism. Furthermore, incarceration can disrupt social support networks and worsen social isolation, making it even more difficult for individuals to access treatment and support upon release.

The risk of death is also significantly increased for individuals with co-occurring substance use and mental health disorders. Substance abuse can lead to overdose, accidents, and other forms of injury or death. Mental health disorders, such as depression and anxiety, can also increase the risk of suicidal behavior and death. Furthermore, individuals with co-occurring disorders are more likely to experience chronic medical conditions, such as heart disease and diabetes, which can also increase the risk of death.

The economic costs of co-occurring substance use, and mental health disorders are also significant. A study by the National Institute of Mental Health estimated that the annual economic burden of co-occurring disorders in the United States is over $100 billion. This includes costs associated with healthcare, incarceration, and lost productivity.

Addiction recovery plans are personalized strategies developed to help individuals overcome addiction and achieve long-term sobriety. These plans are typically created with the help of a healthcare professional, therapist, or addiction specialist. The goal of the plan is to address the physical, emotional, and psychological aspects of addiction.

There are various treatment styles for addiction recovery, including inpatient, outpatient, and residential programs. Inpatient programs provide 24/7 care and supervision in a hospital or clinical setting. Outpatient programs offer flexible scheduling and treatment sessions on a part-time basis. Residential programs provide a supportive community and immersive treatment experience.

The treatment process typically begins with an initial assessment and evaluation. This is followed by detoxification, which can be medically supervised to ensure safety and comfort. After detox, individuals participate in therapy sessions, such as cognitive-behavioral therapy (CBT) or group therapy. Medications like methadone or buprenorphine may be prescribed to manage withdrawal symptoms or cravings. Family therapy and counseling are also essential components of the treatment process.

The minimum time required for results varies depending on individual circumstances and treatment plans. Research suggests that at least 90 days of treatment is necessary for significant improvement. However, some individuals may require longer treatment durations, such as 6-12 months.

Alternative treatment plans may include holistic approaches like acupuncture, yoga, or meditation. Nutritional therapy and fitness programs can also support recovery. Some individuals may benefit from animal-assisted therapy or art therapy.

Sober living homes play a crucial role in supporting individuals during the recovery process. These homes provide a safe, supportive community and structured environment. Residents typically participate in household chores, attend therapy sessions, and engage in community activities.

Sober living homes offer numerous benefits, including increased accountability and support. Residents can develop essential life skills, such as budgeting and job searching. Sober living homes also provide a sense of community and belonging.

The federal law for operating a sober living home is governed by the Fair Housing Act (FHA). The FHA requires that sober living homes comply with specific regulations, such as providing reasonable accommodations for individuals with disabilities. Sober living homes must also adhere to local zoning laws and ordinances.

Accreditation is essential for sober living homes to ensure quality care and services. The National Alliance for Recovery Residences (NARR) provides accreditation for sober living homes. Accreditation demonstrates a commitment to providing safe, supportive, and effective care.

Peer support plays a vital role in the recovery process, particularly in sober living homes. Peer support specialists provide guidance, encouragement, and support to residents. Peer support can help individuals develop coping skills, manage cravings, and maintain sobriety.

Family involvement is crucial in the recovery process, particularly during the early stages. Family members can provide emotional support, encouragement, and accountability. Family therapy can also help individuals develop healthy communication patterns and relationships.

Relapse prevention is an essential component of the recovery process. Individuals can develop relapse prevention plans, which include strategies for managing cravings and avoiding triggers. Regular therapy sessions and support group meetings can also help individuals maintain sobriety.

Becoming a substance abuse counselor in America typically requires a bachelor's degree in a field such as psychology, sociology, or counseling. However, many substance abuse counselors hold master's degrees or higher. According to the Bureau of Labor Statistics, the typical educational requirement for substance abuse counselors is a bachelor's degree, although some employers may prefer or require a master's degree. In addition to formal education, substance abuse counselors must also complete a certain number of hours of supervised clinical experience and pass a certification exam.

The certification exam for substance abuse counselors varies by state, but most states require counselors to pass the National Certified Addiction Counselor (NCAC) exam or the Certified Addiction Counselor (CAC) exam. The NCAC exam is administered by the National Certification Commission for Addiction Professionals (NCC AP), while the CAC exam is administered by the International Certification and Reciprocity Consortium (IC&RC).

In contrast, becoming a mental health counselor or therapist in America typically requires a master's degree in a field such as counseling, psychology, or social work. According to the Bureau of Labor Statistics, the typical educational requirement for mental health counselors is a master's degree. In addition to formal education, mental health counselors must also complete a certain number of hours of supervised clinical experience and pass a licensure exam.

The licensure exam for mental health counselors varies by state, but most states require counselors to pass the National Clinical Mental Health Counselor Examination (NCMHCE) or the National Counselor Examination (NCE). The NCMHCE and NCE are administered by the National Board for Certified Counselors (NBCC) (NBCC, 2020).

The cost of becoming a substance abuse counselor or mental health counselor in America can vary depending on the location, institution, and program. However, according to the Council for Accreditation of Counseling and Related Educational Programs (CACREP), the average cost of a master's degree program in counseling is around $20,000 per year.

In contrast, the cost of becoming a substance abuse counselor or mental health counselor in other countries can be significantly lower. For example, in the United Kingdom, the cost of a master's degree program in counseling or psychotherapy can range from £5,000 to £10,000 per year.

In Australia, the cost of a master's degree program in counseling or psychotherapy can range from AU$20,000 to AU$30,000 per year. In Canada, the cost of a master's degree program in counseling or psychotherapy can range from CAD$10,000 to CAD$20,000 per year.

The process of becoming a substance abuse counselor or mental health counselor in other countries can also vary significantly. For example, in the United Kingdom, substance abuse counselors must complete a diploma or certificate program in counseling or psychotherapy, as well as a certain number of hours of supervised clinical experience.

In Australia, substance abuse counselors must complete a

bachelor's or master's degree program in counseling or psychother-apy, as well as a certain number of hours of supervised clinical experience. In Canada, substance abuse counselors must complete a diploma or certificate program in counseling or psychotherapy, as well as a certain number of hours of supervised clinical experience.

In terms of certification, the requirements can also vary significantly depending on the country. For example, in the United Kingdom, substance abuse counselors can become certified through the UK Council for Psychotherapy (UKCP), while in Australia, substance abuse counselors can become certified through the Australian Counseling Association (ACA).

In Canada, substance abuse counselors can become certified through the Canadian Counseling and Psychotherapy Association (CCPA) (CCPA, 2020). In the United States, substance abuse counselors can become certified through the National Certification Commission for Addiction Professionals (NCC AP) or the International Certification and Reciprocity Consortium (IC&RC).

CHAPTER 9

CONCLUSION: THE WORLD NEEDS YOU

"Indeed, Allah will not change the condition of a people until they change what is in themselves. And when Allah intends for a people ill, there is no repelling it. And there is not for them besides Him any patron.".
-Holy Quran, Surah Ar-Rad (13:11)

Substance abuse and alcohol addiction have deeply shaped my life, not only through personal experiences but also through my professional work and global observations. Growing up surrounded by addiction, I witnessed firsthand how substance use disorders can devastate individuals and families, creating cycles of trauma and dysfunction that are difficult to break. My father's struggles with drug addiction and my grandmother's battle with alcoholism were two of the most significant factors in shaping my understanding of addiction. Watching my grandmother's health deteriorate due to alcohol use was one of the most painful experiences of my life, and it forced me to confront the harsh realities of addiction from an early age.

As I traveled the world, I realized that substance abuse is not just an American issue—it is a global crisis. No matter where I went, I saw the same patterns of addiction, poverty, and systemic failure. Substance use disorders are not limited to one race, nationality, or socioeconomic class; they impact people from all walks of life. Yet, despite the universal nature of addiction, I noticed that different countries handle the problem in vastly different ways. While some nations focus on harm reduction and rehabilitation, others, like the United States, continue to rely on punitive measures that disproportionately affect marginalized communities.

The so-called War on Drugs, launched by Presidents Nixon, Reagan, and Clinton, has had devastating consequences, particularly for Black and Brown communities. What was initially framed as an effort to reduce drug use became a tool for mass incarceration. The policies enacted under these administrations, such as mandatory minimum sentences and the disparity between crack and powder cocaine sentencing, have led to the disproportionate imprisonment of African Americans and Latinos. Instead of addressing addiction as a public health issue, the government criminalized it, tearing families apart and perpetuating cycles of poverty and incarceration.

One of the most tragic consequences of the War on Drugs is the impact it has had on fatherless children. When fathers are incarcerated for nonviolent drug offenses, their children are left to navigate life without paternal guidance. According to the attachment theory, children need secure emotional bonds with their caregivers to develop into healthy, well-adjusted adults. However, when fathers are removed from their children's lives due to incarceration, it often results in emotional distress, behavioral problems, and an increased likelihood of engaging in criminal activity themselves. This cycle of fatherlessness and incarceration continues to devastate communities of color across the country.

My own experiences with the criminal justice system have further solidified my understanding of its flaws. Being falsely arrested and falsely accused of possessing drugs opened my eyes to the injustices that many Black men face. Racial profiling and wrongful convictions are disturbingly common, and many individuals are forced to fight legal battles simply because of the color of their skin. My experience, though painful, gave me a deeper appreciation for those who endure these injustices on a much larger scale.

Working in law enforcement, I also saw how deeply ingrained substance abuse is within correctional institutions. Many people assume that prisons are drug-free environments, but in reality, drugs are widely available behind bars. Corrupt staff members, smuggling operations, and the demand for narcotics create an underground economy that thrives within correctional facilities. This further complicates the issue of rehabilitation, as individuals struggling with addiction often continue their substance use while incarcerated, making it even harder for them to reintegrate into society once released.

Despite these systemic issues, I firmly believe that there is a way forward. One of the most effective ways to combat substance abuse and addiction is through education and counseling. Becoming a substance abuse and alcohol addiction counselor has allowed me to help others break the chains of addiction and regain control of their lives. Recovery is possible, but it requires comprehensive support systems, access to mental health services, and a shift in societal attitudes toward addiction. We must move away from punishment and toward treatment if we truly want to make a difference.

The lessons I have learned through my personal journey, my travels, and my career have shaped my commitment to advocacy. I believe that policy reform, community support, and education are key to addressing the addiction crisis. If we continue to criminalize addiction without addressing its root causes, we will never break the cycle. Instead, we need to invest in mental health services, rehabilitation programs, and economic opportunities that give people a real chance at recovery.

Furthermore, we must acknowledge the generational trauma caused by substance abuse and incarceration. Families like mine have been deeply affected by addiction, and it is our responsibility to ensure that future generations do not suffer the same fate. Healing starts with recognizing the mistakes of the past and taking proactive steps to create a better future. This means advocating for criminal justice reform, supporting policies that prioritize rehabilitation over incarceration, and working to dismantle the racial disparities that have plagued the War on Drugs from its inception.

Through my experiences, I have come to understand addiction as more than just a personal struggle—it is a societal issue that requires collective action. The stigma surrounding addiction prevents many individuals from seeking help, and the lack of resources makes recovery even more challenging. If we want to see real change, we must shift our approach from punishment to compassion. Addiction is not a moral failing; it is a disease, and it should be treated as such.

Looking back on my life, I see a story of resilience, pain, and redemption. I have witnessed the worst aspects of addiction, but I have also seen the power of recovery. I have watched loved ones succumb to their addictions, but I have also helped others reclaim their lives. My journey has taught me that while addiction can destroy, recovery can rebuild.

As I move forward, I am committed to using my voice to advocate for change. Whether through counseling, writing, or community work, I will continue to fight for those affected by substance abuse and mass incarceration. I hope that my story serves as both a warning and an inspiration—a testament to the destructive power of addiction, but also to the strength of the human spirit.

The fight against addiction is far from over, but I remain hopeful. By addressing the root causes of substance abuse, reforming our criminal justice system, and providing real support to those in need, we can break the cycle and create a future where addiction does not define our communities. This is not just my fight—it is a fight for all of us.

Ultimately, my story is one of survival, perseverance, and purpose. I refuse to let addiction, incarceration, or systemic injustice define my life. Instead, I choose to be a force for change, using my experiences to help others navigate their own struggles. The road ahead is long, but I am ready to walk it, step by step, with hope, determination, and unwavering belief in the possibility of a better future.

I want my name to be placed in the history books alongside the likes of Malcolm X, Fred Hampton, Martin Luther King Jr., and Alexander Crummell—men who dedicated their lives to fighting for justice, uplifting their communities, and challenging oppressive systems. These men understood that true leadership is not about personal gain but about sacrificing for the greater good. They spoke truth to power, mobilized people toward change, and left legacies that continue to inspire generations. Like them, I want my life's work to be a testament to resilience, advocacy, and the relentless pursuit of justice.

Malcolm X taught us the importance of self-empowerment, education, and the right to defend our dignity. Fred Hampton showed us the power of unity and community organizing, proving that change is possible when people come together with a shared vision. Martin Luther King Jr. gave us the blueprint for nonviolent resistance and the unwavering belief that justice will prevail. Alexander Crummell championed Black intellectualism, urging us to embrace education and uplift our people. Their legacies have shaped the world we live in, and I refuse to let my contributions go unnoticed. I want my story to stand as a continuation of their fight—a modern-day testament that the struggle for justice and equity is far from over.

My mission is bigger than me; it is about ensuring that future generations have the tools, knowledge, and inspiration to break the cycles of addiction, mass incarceration, and systemic oppression. I want my name to be etched into history as someone who did not just witness injustice but actively fought against it. Through my experiences, my writing, my counseling, and my advocacy, I strive to be a voice for the voiceless, a guide for those lost in the darkness, and a living example of what it means to rise above adversity.

When history reflects on my life, I want it to say that I was a warrior for my people, a champion for those society tried to forget, and a man who used every ounce of his strength to make a difference. I want my story to be studied, my words to be quoted, and my work to be continued long after I am gone. I refuse to be just another statistic, or another name lost in time. I will be remembered, not just for surviving but for leading, inspiring, and changing the world—just as the greats before me did.

"Your past does not define your future, but the lessons you have learned along the way shape the person you are becoming. Every struggle, every setback, and every moment of pain has prepared you for something greater. You are

not a victim of your circumstances—you are a survivor, a warrior, and a beacon of hope for those who come after you. The weight of generational trauma may rest on your shoulders, but you have the power to break the cycle. You have the strength to heal, to rise, and to rebuild. Let your story be a testament to resilience, a message to the world that no matter how many times life knocks you down, you will stand again. Keep pushing, keep fighting, and keep believing—because your purpose is bigger than your pain, and your future is waiting for you to claim it."

Bibliography

AARP Foundation.(2020). Loneliness and social isolation.

Ainsworth, M. D. S.(1978). Patterns of attachment: A psychological study of the strange situation. Lawrence Erlbaum.

Ainsworth, M. D. S., Blehar, M. C., Waters, E., & Wall, S.(1978). Patterns of attachment: A psychological study of the strange situation. Lawrence Erlbaum.

Alexander, M.(2010). The new Jim Crow: Mass incarceration in the age of colorblindness. The New Press.

American Correctional Association.(2020). Corrections: The human side.

American Heart Association.(2017). Alcohol and heart health.

American Liver Foundation.(2020). Alcohol-related liver disease.

American Psychological Association.(2020). Attachment theory and research. https://www.apa.org/news/press/releases/stress/2020/attachment-theory

American Psychological Association.(2020). Substance use and addiction. https://www.apa.org

American Society of Addiction Medicine.(2020). The ASAM essentials of addiction medicine.

American Society on Aging.(2020).

Bowlby, J.(1969). Attachment and loss: Vol. 1. Attachment. Basic Books.

Bureau of Justice Statistics.(1997). Prison and jail inmates at midyear 1997. U.S. Department of Justice. https://bjs.ojp.gov/content/pub/pdf/pjim97.pdf

Bureau of Justice Statistics.(2020). Correctional officers.

Cassidy, J., & Shaver, P. R.(Eds.). (2016). Handbook of attachment: Theory, research, and clinical applications (3rd ed.). Guilford Press.

Centers for Disease Control and Prevention.(2019). Excessive drinking.

Centers for Disease Control and Prevention.(2020). Drug overdose deaths.

Centers for Disease Control and Prevention.(2020). Liver disease.

Centers for Disease Control and Prevention.(2022). Alcohol use and your health.

Centers for Disease Control and Prevention.(2022). Substance use disorders.

Child Welfare Information Gateway.(2019). Substance abuse and child welfare.

DrugAbuse.com.(n.d.). The 20 countries with the harshest drug laws in the world.   https://drugabuse.com/blog/the-20-countries-with-the-harshest-drug-laws-in-the-world/

Duster, T.(1997). The war on drugs: The cultural and economic context. In Race, class, and gender in the United States. Macmillan.

Ehrlichman, J.(1994). Interview with Dan Baum.Harper's Magazine. Retrieved from https://harpers.org/archive/2016/04/legalize-it-all/

Firestone, L.(2012). How your attachment styleimpacts your relationships.Psychology Today. https://www.psychologytoday.com/us/blog/compassion-matters/201202/how-your-attachment-style-impacts-your-relationships

GAO.(2019). Nursing home care.

Goode, E., & Ben-Yehuda, N.(2009). Moral panics: The social construction of deviance. Wiley-Blackwell.

Hansen, H., & Roberts, M.(2017). Substance abuse and mental health.Journal of Addiction Medicine, 11(5), 381–388.

Holt-Lunstad, J., et al.(2015). Social relationships and mortality risk.

Human Rights Watch.(2000). Punishment and prejudice: Racial disparities in the war on drugs. https://www.hrw.org/reports/2000/usa/

Krieger, N., et al.(2018). Neighborhood socioeconomic deprivation.Social Science & Medicine, 196, 203–211.

LaVeist, T. A., & Wallace, J. M.(2000). Health risk behaviors.Journal of Urban Health, 77(3), 361–373.

Mauer, M., & Huling, T.(1995). Young Black Americans and the criminal justice system: Five years later.The Sentencing Project. https://www.sentencingproject.org/publications/young-black-americans-and-the-criminal-justice-system-five-years-later/

Mayo Clinic.(2022). Alcohol use disorder.

McCoy, A. W.(2003). The politics of heroin: CIA complicity in the global drug trade. Lawrence Hill Books.

Mikulincer, M., & Shaver, P. R.(2012). An attachment perspective on psychopathology.World Psychiatry, 11(1), 11-15. https://doi.org/10.1016/j.wpsyc.2012.01.003

Murray, J., & Farrington, D. P.(2005). Parental imprisonment: Effects on boys' antisocial behaviour and delinquency through the life-course.Journal of Child Psychology and Psychiatry, 46(12), 1261-1271.

National Cancer Institute.(2020). Alcohol and cancer risk.

National Center on Elder Abuse.(2020). Elder abuse prevalence.

National Council on Aging.(2020).

National Helpline.(2020). 1-800-662-HELP(4357).

National Highway Traffic Safety Administration.(n.d.). Drive sober or get pulled over. U.S. Department of Transportation.

National Institute of Justice.(2019). Corrections.

National Institute of Mental Health.(2020). Depression.

National Institute on Alcohol Abuse and Alcoholism.(2020). Understanding alcohol use disorder.

National Institute on Drug Abuse.(2020). Economic costs of substance abuse.

National Institute on Drug Abuse.(2020). Substance abuse and addiction. https://www.drugabuse.gov

Nixon, R.(1971). Remarks about an intensified program for drug abuse prevention and control.The American Presidency Project. Retrieved from https://www.presidency.ucsb.edu/documents/remarks-about-intensified-program-for-drug-abuse-prevention-and-control

Poehlmann, J.(2005). Children's experiences.

Provine, D. M.(2007). Unequal under law: Race in the war on drugs. University of Chicago Press.

Roosevelt University.(2014). Race, drugs, and policing: Understanding disparities in drug arrests.Institute for Metropolitan Affairs. https://www.roosevelt.edu/ima

SAMHSA.(2020). National survey on substance abuse.

Shlafer, R. J., & Poehlmann, J.(2010). Attachment matters.

Simpson, J. A., & Rholes, W. S.(2017). Adult attachment, stress, and romantic relationships.Current Opinion in Psychology, 13, 19-24. https://doi.org/10.1016/j.copsyc.2016.04.006

Substance Abuse and Mental Health Services Administration.(2022). Treatment locator.

The Addiction Recovery Guide.(2020).

The Holy Bible.(2011). Malachi 4:6 (New International Version). Zondervan.

The Holy Quran.(n.d.). Surah Al-Baqarah – 2:156 (S. Saheeh, Trans.).

The Holy Quran.(n.d.). Surah Al-Hajj – 22:46 (S. Saheeh, Trans.).

Tonry, M.(1995). Malign neglect: Race, crime, and punishment in America. Oxford University Press.

UNODC.(2020). World drug report.

Vera Institute of Justice.(2002). The growth of incarceration in the United States: Exploring causes and consequences. https://www.vera.org/publications/the-growth-of-incarceration-in-the-united-states

WHO.(2018). Global status report on alcohol and health.

World Health Organization.(2020). Substance abuse. https://www.who.int

Wituk, S., et al.(2012). Community support.Journal of Community Psychology, 40(1), 39–53.

* 9 7 9 8 8 9 6 9 1 7 6 1 8 *